# ACCOUNTABLE
## THE JOSEPH USHER STORY

*A GREAT GRAND DAUGHTER REVEALS*
*THE TRUTH ABOUT HER FAMILY'S*
*SECRET, TROUBLED PAST*

BY
NANCY PANOCH

3-9-13

To Anetta,
Enjoy my
book and tell
me who you think
did it, is always so
it is always so
nice to see you at
Petite Salon with Ben.
Panoch

D1409851

Publisher: Expert Subjects
4775 Collins Avenue, suite 3206
Miami Beach, FL 33140

Disclaimer: Every effort has been made to make this book as complete
and accurate as possible. While the publisher and author of this book
have used their best efforts in preparing this book, they make no repre-
sentations or warranties with respect to the accuracy or completeness of
the factual information and contents of this book. Therefore, the author
and publisher shall have neither liability nor responsibility to any person
or entity for any loss or damage caused, or alleged to have been caused,
directly or indirectly, by the information contained in this book.

The Joseph Usher Story

An Expert Subjects' book, published by
agreement with the author

ISBN 978-0-9886765-1-0

Library of Congress Cataloging-in-Publication Data
p. cm. 1. United States. Navy. SEALs—Fiction. 2. Improvised explo-
sive devices—Fiction. 3. Iran—Fiction. 4. Terrorism—Fiction. I. Title.
PS3623.I5639 C66 2013 813—dc23

Cover design by Jason Alexander

Expert Subjects, LLC

*This book is for my family.*

*I feel this story needed to be told.*
*In this telling I hope to bring understanding to our*
*family history, and uncover this mysterious crime from*
*our past that was kept a secret from us all.*

## ACKNOWLEDGMENTS

*First, I want to thank my Aunt Carol and Uncle Leland since
their work on our genealogy made my telling of this story possible.
Thank you to my husband Ron, and our children
William and Susie Sudah, Karen Panoch, Gary and Christine Panoch for all your encouragement.*

*My new author friends Gwen Ramsey and Virginia Crane
helped to guide me from the beginning. I have appreciated their
advice and motivation to keep writing.*

*I thank my Petite Beauty Salon Girls, Cilene, Diane, Michelle,
Annette, and Sandra. They have supported me through this process
as well as my neighbor, Ann, who scanned the pages. I say thank
you both Cilene and Jeriel, my computer specialists who saved me
many times and helped me with my computer skills.*

*Last but not least I thank my mother who helped so much by
sharing my grandmother's stories of her childhood. For my
mother, this is a sad story, but for me, it is an illumination
of my grandmother's life.*

# Foreword

Dear Readers,

I begin with love in my heart. There is a true story I wish to share with you. In 1903, in Cedar Rapids, Iowa, there was a mysterious murder that involved my great-grandparents, Joseph and Lucy Usher. This tragic event has affected my family from the moment it occurred, and on into the following decades of each generation to this day.

Several years ago my mother, for the first time, told me about our Native American ancestry. My son, who was a youngster at the time, was fascinated, but my mother never mentioned it again, since she really was not that informed about our genealogy, so we let this topic go.

However, a few years later, I discovered more about it from my Aunt Carol Litterer and Uncle Leland Blanchard. They had been working hard on our family's genealogy, and in the course of their research, they discovered the family secret. They were the ones who first whispered of the concealed murder story, which was written on one scant sheet, nestled in the family history. This was all I knew, and I didn't think we would ever learn any more, so once more I let it go.

Then three years ago, my son called to ask how closely we are related to the Native Americans. He was also curious about the murder, so I told him that I would work on this family mystery. I phoned Aunt Carol and she told me how my Aunt and Uncle had gone to the Cedar Rapids' newspapers and retrieved articles regarding the murder. Additionally, they attended the Usher reunions to learn more from family members who knew about this event. Aunt Carol kindly mailed me the newspaper articles as well as a copy of Otto Usher's 1965 hand-written life story. His children had requested he write his memoir before he died, and between his personal account, and a complete Usher family history, I learned who was believed to have committed the murder.

Due to my son's prodding, I found myself deep into a family murder mystery story I now feel compelled to tell.

Most of all, this story is a window into the past. With this accumulated knowledge, I have come to know and love my family. My wish is that you, the readers come to love these characters as I do. I have attempted telling this story as true to the facts that I have been so generously given. Now I would like to introduce you to the Usher family and the events that lead up to that fatal and stormy evening in 1903.

## The Joseph Usher Family History

Rachel Cops Usher wiped the tears from her eyes, as she spoke in a quiet Scottish brogue, telling many of her hopes and fears to her husband, John, in 1799 Dublin, Ireland. Rachel had prepared herself to say goodbye to her two courageous sons, Joseph, twenty-one years of age, and Aaron C. who was a mere fifteen. This preparation did not stop the shiver as she handed each his packed bag with provisions carefully chosen to last three months.

The journey to America, by way of Nova Scotia, would be trying, and the Usher family understood Joseph and Aaron would never again set foot on the soil of Ireland. They were determined for their sons to have a better life than their continent afforded. The brothers kissed their mother on each of her cheeks, and hugged her with the realization they would never wrap their arms around her again. John shook each of his son's hands, remembering how he had taught them as young boys to do so with a grip that was neither too powerful nor too soft. Then he, too, hugged his boys. The parents watched as their familiar sons, with shiny black hair and blue eyes, walked away for the last time, but not before promising to lead decent lives and to write as often as they could. Rachel was counting on these promises.

After an arduous journey sailing across the ocean, a trip that seemed to last an eternity, the Usher brothers debarked in Nova Scotia, Canada. Joseph and Aaron had grown to be the best of friends, and this was a blessing, because their survival depended on their brotherly bond. Soon they migrated south to New York City, which seemed a world away from

Dublin, so far from where they had been raised by their adoring parents. Joseph had no idea that his future wife, Ruby Mosokweto, was living in this bustling city and they were soon to meet.

Ruby Mosokweto was from the Winnebago or Algonquin tribe. She could barely remember the day when her Native American family had left her two sisters, her brother and herself at a church in Vermont. This happened so long ago, the painful memory was shrouded. If she shut her eyes, Ruby could faintly conjure the vision of the white wooden church surrounded by leafy trees as well as the ache in her heart. Sadly, her brother ran away, and was never seen again, which left just Ruby, Sarah (Soketo), and Qwasito who were adopted by the Nichols, an English family.

The sisters grew up with kindness and English culture; however, their Native American heritage remained strong, especially in regards to their birth language, which they continued to speak no matter how many years passed. When Ruby and Sarah were grown, they traveled together to New York City to find work and begin their new lives. Just as Joseph and Aaron found comfort in their friendship, so did Ruby and Sarah lend one another support and love.

The day Joseph first noticed Ruby, such a pretty young Native American woman, his heart raced. "I'm going to talk to her," he said to his brother, Aaron, and talk to her he did. Ruby and Joseph's life together began that day; they were married sometime around 1800, and they along with her two sisters and Aaron, settled near Clarence, in New York. This happy young couple was also graced by all of their Native American friends living nearby.

Around 1814, Aaron and Sara, Ruby's sister, were married. Qwasito never married, but remained with the Usher family and helped with the raising of their children. Eventually, Joseph, Ruby, Aaron and Sarah along with their growing families, moved from New York State to Ohio in the years between 1816 and 1820. They made this slow and trying journey by oxen and wagons and were accompanied by forty Native Americans.

The years passed by in Ohio. Joseph and Ruby had a son they named Joseph–who was called Joel–the seventh child born to them in 1820. He was the second son the couple had named Joseph; this was a custom, the first child by this name had died quite young. The first child, Willard, was thrown from a horse at the age of twenty and killed. Sadly, the last child born to Ruby in Ohio, also named Willard, died, at the age of twelve. These were hard times and it was not uncommon to bury many a child.

Around 1837 Joseph and Ruby, Aaron and Sarah, along with their families, once again moved. This time they headed for Iowa, which had not yet even become a state. At the time, Joseph was fifty-nine years of age, and Aaron was fifty-three. The two families settled in Cedar Rapids, or Linn County, and consequently, Joseph is listed in the county registry as "an early settler in Monroe Township." One of the Ushers is also cited as having filed for a territorial deed to land in Linn County, which he successfully obtained. The land the Usher's settled was not relinquished by the Sac and Fox tribes until 1837, and in approximately 1838, the Dubuque Land Office opened. When the Ushers choose to settle in Cedar Rapids, there were only one or two cabins, and the land was said to be full of rascals and horse thieves. Not until December 29, 1846, did Iowa became the twenty-ninth state in the Union, an indication of how rough it must have been for new settlers to carve out a safe and prosperous life for themselves.

Joseph and his brother were blacksmiths by trade, but the family also ran many other businesses in the Cedar Rapids area in order to thrive, such as a ferry they operated on the Cedar River. Additionally, the Ushers were also farmers, brick makers, and bricklayers. The Usher family became a powerful force by staying together, working together, and building a successful community.

When the Ushers moved to Iowa, Joseph Aaron Usher Sr., or Joel, who was born on February 20, 1820, was about seventeen years old. Joel was a handsome young man, with the Native American half of his heritage coming out strongly in his appearance. In 1844, at the age of twenty-four, he was married to Lydia Williams. Lydia was a lovely young woman who, sadly, died in childbirth. Joel then married Lydia's sister, Harriet Williams, in 1848, and like her sister before her, poor Harriet died due to childbirth. Joel Usher experienced great sadness in his life as his third wife, Mary Amboy, died in 1850, after giving birth to their son, Joseph Aaron Usher Jr.

In 1854, Isaac P. Usher, his mother unknown was born. Not for ten years did Joel find another love. This time he married Joanne Wiltsey in 1860. Baby William Henry Usher was born on August 20, 1861 and finally both mother and son were healthy and thriving. All seemed to be well. Joseph Aaron Jr. was fifteen at the time, and his little half-brother, William, only four. However, tragedy struck again. Joel became suddenly ill and died at the age of forty-five in 1865.

Joanne could not support both boys by herself. Joseph Aaron Jr. found himself parentless, with nowhere to go. Fortunately for the boy, neighbors took him into their home, and took it upon themselves to educate him with reading, writing and math. On September 29, 1843, Joseph's Native American Grandmother, Ruby, died, and on October 1, 1848 his Irish Grandfather, Joseph Usher died. Ruby is buried in Iowa City and her husband Joseph is buried in Cedar Rapids.

Joseph Aaron Usher Jr. was one-quarter Native American, and he was known to be a little different. He was a loner who ran on nervous energy, perhaps due to the fact that he had lost both his parents at such a young age. Joseph worked for his room and board. Hard work was what he understood, and he also knew how to be on good terms with the people he knew in Cedar Rapids. Then Joseph met Mary Suzanna Peal, and his outlook on life changed, as love so often has the effect. Mary Suzanna Peal had come from England in 1864 at the age of seven years old. She was petite, pretty and perky, and had many attributes Joseph adored and admired as well as the culture, class and nature he so badly needed. Meeting this young woman set Joseph on a path to success, along with his strong work ethic. They married on January 20, 1873, when Joseph was twenty-three and Mary was a young seventeen.

On December 1, 1874, a baby girl, Mary Jane, and known as Jennie, was born. Two years later, a second baby was born but died; baby George Arthur was born July 9, 1878 four years after his sister, Jennie, and Otto Cecil was born eight years later November 21, 1886.

Around the time Joseph married Mary, he also purchased his hundred-acre farm on which he began a milking herd of cattle delivering milk to the creamery. When Otto was small, his father began a milk route, delivering to homes and businesses in Cedar Rapids. In time, Joseph and his boys were milking thirty cows, and supplied milk every day to the community. Otto was nine years old when he began helping with chores; he recollected that his father would yelp like a wolf to awaken his boys when it was time to begin chores on cold, dark mornings. Otto also recollected a normal and happy childhood.

Jennie was married March 22, 1893, and moved to Chicago with her husband, Percy Dudley. The two had met when Percy had arrived from England, and he spent time living with the Usher family to learn the customs of living in America. Percy was the third young man the Usher's had hosted. Jennie and Percy eventually had two sons.

After Jennie was gone, baby Walter Earl was born to Joseph and Mary on April 23, 1894, just eight years after Otto, who was thrilled to be a big brother to such a cute baby boy. George was not as happy, and believed the birth of Walter was completely unnecessary.

When Mary fell ill, her husband did all he could to obtain good medical help. The local doctor recommended surgery, and Mary was frightened by this prospect. Joseph did the smart thing and took his wife to Chicago for a second opinion. They stayed with Jennie and her family while seeking the additional medical advice. However, much to Mary's dismay, the doctors in Chicago also recommended surgery. Mary was considered a brave woman, but she could not face having surgery.

Otto was twelve when he remembered his mother being ill. In the late spring and summer the boys would carry their ailing mother and placed her in George's top buggy. The boys would then pull the buggy by hand to the garden so their mother could watch her children tending the vegetables. Soon, however, the end came for Mary, with all the sadness attending her death. Little Walter was not even five years old when his mother died at the age of forty-one on August 6, 1898.

It was said that Joseph began to see someone very soon, less than a year after Mary's death. The family voiced their disapproval, even though they admitted that Joseph had done all he could for his wife. There was no doubt in anyone's mind that Joseph had loved Mary.

Joseph's stepmother, Joanne Usher and Grandmother Steadman, arrived to help his family in their time of sorrow and crisis. George by this time was working away from home and was nearly farming on his own. Short on help and with the milk business growing, Joseph often hired help. He turned to both farm hands and domestic hands, and due to this need for assistance, Joseph became acquainted with William Garrity. Garrity worked for room, board and a dollar a day. Joseph picked him up in town, brought him back to the property on the milk wagon, and Garrity stayed for as long as he was needed.

Joseph met Lucy Jane Gillis and her sister, Hulda, in the home of Reverend and Mrs. Lockwood. Reverend Lockwood was pastor of the St. Paul's Methodist Church, in Cedar Rapids. Mrs. Lockwood employed Lucy. Lucy was twenty-three, and Joseph fifty years old when they married.

Her new family did not accept Lucy. When Joseph brought his pretty young bride home, George found reason to resent her though he tolerated and accepted her presence in a half-hearted way. Otto and Walter were more cooperative, and Otto, in particular, felt his new stepmother was to be pitied not blamed.

Each summer Jennie and her two boys came from Chicago to visit Cedar Rapids. Jennie was sweet in attempting to make her father's new bride feel as welcomed into the family as possible. Lucy had other support as well–a neighbor, Mrs. Weed, who came by to visit her, and Lucy was known to return the visit on occasion. For these trips, Joseph bought Lucy a new open buggy to make her getting about easier, but she didn't make that much use of it, only occasionally visiting her Uncle and Aunt in Cedar Rapids.

Unfortunately, many folks felt that Joseph should have married someone closer to his age and his life experiences than he and Lucy. If Joseph had selected a better–suited wife, all may have turned out differently. A year after Lucy and Joseph married, it became apparent that she was having mental trouble of some kind. Occasionally she would become almost uncontrollable, then the spell would pass and for several weeks she would appear to be quite normal again. Lucy was as pleasant as anyone.

During this time, George and his father, Joseph, were in a farming partnership together. On February 5, 1902 George Arthur Usher married Violet Hansen. Soon he and his wife would move to Chickasaw County in North East Iowa. Otto was a fifteen-year old young man and was very involved with the farm work himself. No one knew the storm clouds that were about to settle over the Usher family and alter the life they had worked so hard to create.

In late fall of 1902, Otto left Cedar Rapids for Chicago. He spent the winter with his sister, Jennie, and his brother-in-law, Percy. Otto was just sixteen and worked hard in the stockyards and then in a jewelry factory. He enjoyed his winter in Chicago, being able to focus on work and evade the problems that had plagued him at home. Otto had grown into a strong and handsome young man with black hair and hazel eyes, leaning toward brown. In the spring, word was sent to Chicago that Otto was needed back on the farm. George had accumulated quite a bit of farm machinery and some horses. This was a great success. Otto returned and helped in the beginning of March 1903, to load up a car at Covington since they were shipping George's things to nearby Ionia. George had rented the Brookings' farm, and he was moving in with Violet with high hopes for a prosperous and happy life.

Therefore, Otto found himself with plenty to do. He found he was content back on the farm, enjoying the country life once more. City life was not what Otto desired anymore. Despite Lucy's depressed periods, Otto and little Walter were getting along with her very well in the spring of 1903. As there was much work to do, with so many cattle, and all the work associated with dairying, Joseph also hired William Garrity, the farm hand who had so often helped. After a two-week period of rain, Joseph brought Garrity back from town, and what took place on Tuesday night, May 26, 1903, still remains a mystery to this day.

## Accountable: The Joseph Usher Story

It was written that nothing that had ever happened in the southeastern part of Linn County–even in the days when horse thieves were hunted down and hanged for horse steal-ing–had ever caused the talk and speculation in this part of the state as much as the murder of William Garrity. The speculation continues to this day. This account will attempt to unearth at last the events that transpired on the property of Joseph and Lucy Usher on that fateful spring night.

# Chapter 1

**Monday, May 25, 1903 Cedar Rapids, Iowa**

Bill Garrity was never so happy to hear footsteps as they reverberated down the planks of the wooden hallway. The footsteps belonged to the heavy boots of the deputy, who appeared to unlock the door of Garrity's jail cell and escort him to the office. Garrity noticed creases on the deputy's face, as if he'd just been woken up from a nap on his desk, and he smiled while signing a big x onto the release form. The deputy cleared his throat, and gave Garrity a stern warning not to show up again and to get himself back to work. Garrity nodded, brushed his hair back with his hand, and placed his old hat on top of his head.

When Garrity stepped outside into the light of day, he was not feeling well. He had suffered one hangover too many, and this time his head and stomach hurt him something awful. The circus had been in town for two weeks, and with its arrival had come too much revelry—Garrity knew if he was going to make it much further in life, he had better cut back on the late nights and the drinking.

He found an empty bench on Main Street, in front of the old Arcade Hotel, and slouched down, his eyes focused on the First Street Restaurant, where Joseph Usher was making his last milk delivery of the day. There was no way Garrity's tired feet could carry him very far, but Usher would give him a ride in the milk wagon as he had done many times before.

Usher smiled when he saw Garrity. They met up about five in the evening, just as the daylight was giving way. Usher didn't know whether he should give Garrity yet another talking to or just keep his mouth shut and save himself the trouble. Today Usher felt sorry for him, and decided that all the lecturing wouldn't make a bit of a difference. What mattered was that Usher needed Garrity's hard work on the farm as soon as the weather cleared.

Garrity climbed up on the milk wagon with a little bit of a wobble. He and Usher agreed upon one thing—after chores he needed a good square meal, and a clean bed to catch up on some much required sleep. The two men headed west out of town as threatening storm clouds brewed in the direction they were traveling. Four miles stretched between them and the farm, and Usher signaled the horses with a tap on the reins. These horses were a strong team Usher relied upon to pull the milk wagon on its daily route, but for now, they were simply bringing two tired, hungry, and silent men home.

# Chapter 2

Young Otto had driven the team of horses and empty wagon from Cedar Rapids. For Otto, there was still a sense of pride as he handled such tasks that only years ago had seemed so out-of-reach, the tasks only a man could handle. He turned the wagon into the driveway that led to the farmyard about seven in the evening on Tuesday, May 26, 1903.

The old one-half story farmhouse always made him feel glad when he returned. That's what home was about and he was grateful. The road was muddy and the sky was darker than it should have been on a spring night. Off on the horizon, Otto found a sea of grey punctuated by frequent strikes of lightening. He knew to be quick, and hustle the horses into the barnyard before the hard rain was to begin again.

Otto had extra impetus to hurry—he was starving and eager to sit down to his stepmother's supper. Lucy was a decent cook, preparing meals on the new kitchen stove Otto's father had bought for his new wife three years ago. He unhitched the horses from the wagon and ran for the farmhouse, planning to change into dry clothes and claim his seat at the table.

By the time Otto had changed his damp clothes, his father, Garrity, and his little brother Walter, were already seated. Garrity looked beat, and he sat patiently, watching Lucy scrape the last bit of their supper from a cast iron skillet with thoroughness. Once Otto took his seat, they began to eat. There was a lack of words, only the sounds of chewing and plates being cleaned. Lucy had reason to feel proud of her cooking. Leftovers were not common, but full and content stomachs were.

When supper was over they finished the evening chores. Everyone had his or her routine and knew it well—even Garrity—since he worked as a farmhand with the Ushers often enough. In this way the chores got done quickly and efficiently, and this made Usher as proud as Lucy was of her new stove and cooking. Otto left his father and Garrity talking at the pump. He couldn't make out what they were saying, but from the sound of it, the farmhand had suffered another rough patch—it showed on his weary face and sounded in his tired voice. One by one the men came in for bed—first Otto, then his father, and finally Garrity. By then the storm had reached the Usher's farm. The sound of the rain on the roof was loud and soothing, and the kerosene lamps kept the dark at bay.

Nine-year-old Walter was tired from a full day of playing and helping with chores. He washed his face and feet with the warm water he ladled from the stove, knowing Lucy did not like him crawling between his clean sheets if he was covered in dirt. After he was washed, he climbed the narrow stairs to the bedroom he and Otto shared, got into his little bed and fell asleep like only a child can—suddenly and without worries or cares.

Lucy had finished her supper chores. The hard day's work had taken its toll on her, and she told her husband she was not feeling well. Usher suggested she retire early and she agreed. She knew her husband would be coming to bed soon and she didn't mind a little time to herself when she was this exhausted.

Otto sat at the kitchen table reading *The Gypsies' Prophecy* while his father read the paper. This was something they did often before bed—it was a quiet way to settle the day and spend a little time together as father and son without the weight of words. Garrity did not join them at the table. He glanced at Usher, his head barely visible above the newspaper, and then went to the front room. Soon Usher's eyes grew tired of reading print in the dim kerosene light, his day had been busy and he needed to rest to begin all over again tomorrow, so he said his good nights and went to the downstairs bedroom to his wife.

Garrity, who had been quiet, came over to Otto who was still reading.

"Say, Otto, do you know if they can do anything with a person? Kill them or anything, for saying something? I heard…someone heard… that I had said something."

"Oh no, Bill," Otto replied. "I'm sure no one will bother you about such a trivial thing as that."

"Let me take your shot gun." Garrity suggested. "I will get in the cellar and they won't get me."

Otto closed his book and looked the farmhand in the eyes. He tried to assure Garrity that he need not be fearful, and that he believed he was disturbed beyond any need. Otto found it impossible to read while Garrity skulked around downstairs. His eyes kept skimming the same paragraph over and over, so he put his book down and watched Garrity gather a pan of water, a lantern, and head up to bed.

A tremor of apprehension passed through Otto, but he ignored it and turned back to his book, until he became lost in the story once again. Around nine-thirty he felt sleepy as the storm gained strength outside their protective farmhouse. On his way up to bed, Otto passed through the corner of Garrity's room and saw the lit lantern, and the pan of water sitting on the old wooden chest by the stair railing.

Otto never remembered the farmhand bringing these things up to bed before, and he wondered if it had anything to do with the unrest Garrity had expressed. Walter was asleep in his bed; Otto could make out the shape of his little brother from the light that shone through from Garrity's room. There was no door that could be closed between the two bedrooms. Otto's bed was welcoming, but he couldn't rid himself of the apprehension that had set in when he talked to Garrity. He had the notion of waking his father, but he knew how much rest was needed, and everything seemed quiet in the house. The day had been long, hot, and full of backbreaking chores. Otto fell asleep while trying to make sense of Garrity's fear, and the lightening, thunder and rain continued on outside in Cedar Rapids.

# Chapter 3

Not long after going to bed, Otto was awakened by his father shaking him. "Ottie! Ottie! Wake up! There's something the matter with Bill. He's dying, I guess."

Otto had the feeling of being disoriented, but he managed to sit up and follow his father into Garrity's room adjoining his, and the first thing he noticed was the farmhand lying on his back on top of the bed covers. Garrity's mouth was overflowing with blood, and in the dim light, with the storm outside, the whole effect was gruesome. Usher rubbed Garrity's feet while Otto reached for the pan of water, still resting by the lit lantern on the old chest. Filling this pan of water was one of the last things Otto had seen this man do just a short time ago, and now here he lay in this disturbing state. Otto saw the blood in Garrity's mouth move just slightly. The young man was certain Garrity was dead within a minute of their entering the room—not that he had had a great deal of experience with death.

His father got Walter from his little bed and carried him downstairs. Otto noticed the time was ten-thirty when they took his little brother away from the tragic room. Usher turned to his son and told him to go down to Spicer's–close neighbors who had a telephone. At the Spicer's, Otto was asked to call a Mr. Tom Gibney who was a relative of Garrity's, although Otto had no understanding of how the two men were related. Otto's second phone call was to be to the coroner in Cedar Rapids.

The night was exceedingly dark, even though some of the rain had lifted, there was still thunder and lightning. Taking the trip to Spicer's and placing these two important calls for his father, was just one more indication that Otto was wearing the responsibilities of a young man. This thought brought him comfort in the unsettling events of the night. He thought of his earlier discussion with Garrity and now the man's alarm seemed to resonate with Otto.

With his horse and his lantern, he made his way in the dark and inhospitable night. He placed the two calls, as requested, and returned home with lightening piercing the sky around him. Otto tried, as best he could, to review and figure out what had just happened at his home. His thoughts were scattered and coming fast.

*My father has hired Bill many times over the past years, knowing he was a good and a hard worker for about a month, but then he'd take off and drink up all his wages. When Bill became broke, he'd be ready to go back to work, vowing he'd never go on a bender again. It seemed that while the spirit is willing, the flesh is weak, and so he would fall again. My father always gave him another try, because he appeared so sincere.*

*Lately we went to work and got the oats put in, hauled out and spread the manure by hand, we repaired fences, we were getting the corn ready to be planted–all has seemed to be going right on the farm except for the rain these past two weeks. Then Bill got restless and decided he had to make a trip to town and sure enough he fell victim to his old habit and he disappeared for two weeks.*

*Then this morning, father was about to start on his milk route and he instructed me to pick out five or six of the best fat hogs for the market. He told me to take the hogs to the packinghouse and sell them–after which I took the check to the bank and cashed it to bring the money home to father. I stowed the gold pieces away in my pocket to keep them safe as I started for home.*

*To my dismay the rainy spell was not yet over and the day was very hot. I proceeded on my way home while it started to rain and thunder and lightening–and how it did pour. I was soon wet. I would not be wetter had I jumped in the river.*

*In due time I arrived home and got into dry clothes, and by that time the rain had ceased for the time being at least. Soon after, father arrived home from the milk route.*

*Yesterday he had Bill with him since he met up with him in town and Bill had no place to go. They would not keep him in jail once he sobered up. Bill had supper and did the evening chores as usual. I could see Bill was in a very melancholy mood with scarcely anything to say. This was unusual for him since he was usually congenial and conversant when in his better form.*

By the time Otto's thoughts stopped flooding, he had arrived back at the farmhouse, and his horse turned—without prompting—into the driveway.

# Chapter 4

Otto brought his horse into the barn, and with his lantern he found his way up to the house. Within an hour's time, Garrity's cousin, Mr. Gibney, arrived at the Usher's and introduced himself to the family.

Joseph asked the visitor, "Mr. Gibney, would you like to go upstairs and see Garrity?

"I don't care to go upstairs," Mr. Gibney replied, "but what did happened?"

"It looks like Bill had a hemorrhage."

They waited for daylight, talking and trying to make themselves as restful as they could under the circumstances.

Dr. W.S. King received a message on Wednesday morning, at approximately one-thirty, from Mr. Gibney of Covington; this was notification of William Garrity's death. He explained that Garrity had been found dead in his bed at the Usher's home, and the family claimed he had died due to a hemorrhage. Mr. Gibney informed Dr. King that Garrity had put in a full day's work on Tuesday, and so far as he knew he had never suffered any type of hemorrhage previously. Since it was storming hard at that hour, Dr. King assured Mr. Gibney that his father, Coroner David W. King, would be coming out to the Usher's first thing in the morning.

Otto and Joseph had the chores nearly done by the time the undertaker arrived.

During all those hours, Otto had many thoughts. He was relieved that Lucy seemed in a normal state of mind, she had held up quite well under the calamity that had befallen her during this crisis.

Otto also reflected upon Garrity. They had worked quite closely together this spring season. Garrity needed someone to confide in, and Otto had become that person. Otto learned that Garrity had been a boilermaker by trade, employed by the Great Western Railway at Oelwein. As a result of this job, and the excessive noise, Garrity was slightly deaf. In any case, Garrity had lost his job, Otto presumed on account of his alcoholic tendencies, which rendered him undependable for his trade.

Garrity had made it no secret from Otto how he would drink, become involved with immoral women, who would manage to get his money away from him, then have him thrown out. Garrity was always struggling financially, always broke. Otto witnessed Garrity's repentance—he saw first hand how Garrity had come to realize how foolish he had been, and heard him vow he would change his ways.

Otto was certain Garrity never attended church, but knew him to be Catholic by faith, without ever having turned to a priest for any type of spiritual guidance. Judging by his physical appearance, Otto believed Garrity was about forty-five or fifty years of age, and despite their age difference, Otto had shared with him many of the events that had recently gone on in his sixteen-year-old life. They had become work friends for sure, even though they were an unlikely pair— a drifter, who had more then likely never been married, or picked up a book to read, and a young steady man.

Mr. Cordy Rank was both coroner and undertaker. He arrived early Wednesday morning at the Usher's farm, accompanied—by Lewis Werner of Cedar Rapids. Werner was also a cousin of Garrity's. With Otto's help they wrapped up Garrity's body, placed him in the back of their wagon, and drove back to town—seemingly the natural thing to do.

Shortly after the coroner left, Joseph went on his milk route, stopping at the Spicer's along the way. Ira Conley was a young man who worked as a hired man at their farm, and Joseph asked him to go help Otto clean up the bedroom where Garrity had died. He gave instructions to burn the old wooden bed- stead, straw tick, and quilts–as they were soaked in blood and unsalvageable.

When Conley arrived at the Usher's farm, he and Otto removed the upstairs window and lowered the bed and other items down. The stairway was far too narrow and this way no blood would get throughout the house. After everything was outside, the two hauled the bed and bedding to a ditch by the road to be burned. Conley returned to the Spicer's when this chore was completed.

Coroner King did exactly as was promised. After a very early breakfast, he left the city for the Usher's farm. He met undertaker Ranck with Lewis Werner within a half mile of the farmhouse; the two were returning to the city with Garrity's body in the wagon. The men exchanged greetings and then undertaker Ranck informed the coroner of the events at the Usher's. Ranck explained that upon arriving at the house they found Garrity's body upstairs. He was lying straight on top of the bed. His right hand was down at his side while his left hand lay over his heart. As far as Ranck could tell, there was no evidence of foul play. The members of the Usher family confirmed this theory in stating that Garrity had died from a hemorrhage. Ranck explained they were on their way to the city since, Garrity's relatives planned to inter his remains in the Kenwood Cemetery.

Mr. King was irritated. He carefully inquired into the condition in which the body of Garrity was found. In addition, he reprimanded Mr. Ranck for having touched and further for removing the man's body. In light of knowing he had been summoned, they should have left Garrity as he was found.

Mr. King returned with the undertaker to the city so they could make a through examination of Garrity's body. In the process of washing the body, Mr. Ranck noticed a blood spot next to the left breast. Upon further investigation, Dr. King found the bullet, a .22 short, which was just beneath the skin in the middle of his back. The bullet had entered the left breast, passed through the left lung, passed down the spinal column and stopped opposite the eighth dorsal vertebrae. Death, Dr. King determined, had resulted from a hemorrhage caused by the gunshot wound. With this information in hand, Coroner King at once filed charges before Justice Rail against Joseph Usher for the murder of William Garrity, to be prepared by County Attorney Mekota. After the post-mortem examination was completed, he returned immediately to the Usher's home.

Coroner King was in a state of disbelief upon his arrival at the farm. He discovered that in the brief time since Garrity's body was removed, the Usher family had burned every vestige of furniture in the bedroom. Even Garrity's clothing, itself, had been added to the fire. Additionally, the floor and woodwork of the room had been cleaned.

Coroner King found Lucy doing her usual morning work and was speaking to her when Otto awoke. He had been sleeping on the old sofa out on the east front porch, too tired after the near all-night vigil to continue chores. Coroner King introduced himself to Otto, and then continued closely interrogating Mrs. Usher, Otto and little Walter. Each one of the Usher's denied any knowledge of Garrity's tragedy. No one had heard any gun shot, and until Joseph called them, they were not aware of anything having transpired.

About this time Ira Conley came back to the Usher farm and informed Mr. King that Otto had recently purchased a target rifle.

"Otto, where do you keep your rifle?" Mr. King questioned.

"It is hanging on the nail over my bed. It's in the room adjoining the one in which Garrity slept."

"Bill has been shot and I want you to fetch the gun," the coroner replied.

"I own two guns. I have a .22 caliber rifle and a shot gun." Otto ran upstairs and could see the .22 rifle was not in its usual place. He came back downstairs and told Mr. King the situation.

Mr. King returned upstairs with Otto and looked around. Otto showed him where he kept the cartridges for his rifle. The coroner took a few and placed them in his pocket, he then looked at the upstairs rooms. "It is very important that we find the rifle," he said.

They all began searching the house and every likely place they could find. Otto and Ira took a walk out to the granary, which was seventy-five-feet from the house. They opened the granary door and stepped inside. This was when Ira noticed the rifle lying to one side near the wall, as if it had been tossed there from the open doorway. This discovery shocked Otto. He identified the rifle as his, and saw it contained an empty shell–a .22 short, then he informed Mr. King that he had no knowledge of how the rifle had come to be in the granary or who had fired it. The coroner asked Lucy and Otto a few more questions, and afterwards remarked that he was afraid a murder had been committed, climbing into his cart and driving back to town.

At this time Otto had formed an opinion. He believed Lucy knew no more about what had happened to Garrity then he knew; however, it was quite obvious that Garrity had not shot himself. He didn't carry the rifle outside to the granary, then walk back upstairs to bed. Otto also felt equally sure that his father had no reason or motive for killing Garrity. Why would he have done such a thing? Had he distrusted Garrity to that extent, all he would have had to do was not hire him. Otto was certain that Garrity didn't have any designs toward Lucy, or he would have been aware of it, and in all his talks with Garrity, he had never shown any il- licit intent towards any respectable women, only the profes- sional unmentionables.

The afternoon passed and by three-thirty Joseph had not come home from his milk route. Otto waited about another hour and decided he had better hitch a horse to Lucy's bug- gy, leave the farm and find his father.

# Chapter 5

After a late dinner, Lucy sat out on the front porch with Walter and his friend, a neighbor boy. She was exhausted from the events of the previous night, the lack of sleep, the high emotions, and all the cleaning that was done that morning.

She rocked wearily in her chair as the boys draped themselves on the front steps. A buggy turned into their driveway, carrying two men dressed in suits. They hopped out and inquired if this was the farm of Joseph Usher.

"Yes," Lucy answered. "How may I help you?"

The two men introduced themselves as a reporter and artist from *The Cedar Rapids Gazette*. They then asked if they could have a look around the place—to which Lucy agreed. Looking at her face, the men could see she was laboring under great mental stress. Her eyes were what showed her state the most; she was pale, and yet she maintained an expression of determination despite the circumstances. The determination indicated that Joseph's wife had no intention of giving out any information concerning the dreadful event that had happened last night, making this farmhouse the scene of one of the most mysterious murders in the history of Linn County. The reporters also noted how young Lucy looked, and they guessed her to be about twenty-six years of age. She was an attractive young woman with black hair, brown eyes and beautiful skin.

The reporters had noticed the farmhouse was a substantial little frame, a story-and-a-half structure. The style was similar to many other houses in the area. Several rods from the house were a small barn, a granary and a vehicle shed.

Lucy could tell by the way the men looked around that they were hoping to see her husband. She told them that Joseph was still on his daily milk route. "I expect he will be home soon." When asked if she would show them the room where Garrity had died, supposedly from a "hemorrhage of the lungs," Lucy agreed to let them inside. Her head noticeably drooped when she led the journalists into her kitchen. They followed her to the doorway that opened to the stairs to Garrity's room. Lucy was careful about what she said; she appeared to be in deep meditation, perhaps so she would not incriminate herself or other members of her family.

A dozen or so steps brought them to the top of the stairway, and a narrow passageway only about two feet in width. A railing ran along the edge of the passage, two or three feet from the floor. They entered the room where Garrity had been murdered, a space eight feet by ten feet, with one little window on the south side and another on the west side. Garrity's bed occupied the greater part of the room.

A row of hooks ran along the west end of the room and above the foot of the bed, upon which Garrity was accustomed to hanging his clothes since the room could not accommodate a wardrobe and there was no closet. The only clothing hanging in the room was a suit of black clothes that Garrity wore when he traveled to town. By the wall was a small wooden chest with clean overalls and blouse. Lucy explained that a telescope grip belonged to her, and these were the only items in the room since everything else had been burned. She told the reporters that they could not stand to see the room in such a condition after Garrity's death, so they cleaned out everything after the undertaker had removed his body.

"We also burned Mr. Garrity's old hats, bandana, handkerchiefs, blouse's, old trousers and old shoes. Everything that belonged to Garrity was carried down out of the house in the morning. After the body was removed we placed everything in the ditch to be burned." Even the bedding and the bedstead were taken from the room and burned up. Every indication of what had happened was gone.

Lucy stood at the top of the stairs with her hand resting on the banister as if she badly needed support.

"If the man was shot, he was not shot in this house," blurted Lucy.

"What kind of a man was Garrity?" the reporter asked her.

"He was a quiet man, but I don't know him well…yes, I did; he worked here off and on for several years but I never had anything to do with him."

While the reporter talked with Lucy the artist moved into the adjoining room where Otto and Walter slept. Their room was twelve by thirteen feet. The large bed on the south side of the room belonged to Otto, while the smaller one on the east side was Walter's. A wall partition separated the room and a doorway with no door; there was a window on the south side and east side of the room. The artist could see a nail between the windows a few feet above the bed where Otto hung his .22-inch long and .22 caliber rifle. Sunday he had hung the rifle there after hunting with a few of the neighborhood boys.

The journalists returned with Lucy downstairs and back to the front porch. They sat as Lucy told them that Joseph had been a dairy farmer for the past twelve or thirteen years, and she could not imagine her husband having committed this crime since the two men had always gotten along well.

The reporters continued their questions. Lucy stuck to the same story she had given to the coroner. "The first we knew about Garrity dying was at half past ten o'clock. We always go to bed early. We all were in bed by nine o'clock. At half past ten, Joseph heard Garrity groaning and he went upstairs and found him dying. I heard the noise about the same time that Joseph did. Joseph woke up Otto. He sent him down to Spicer's to telephone Garrity's cousin at Covington. He was to tell him to come out to the farm quickly, for Bill was dying. Bill's cousin came right away. Then they telephoned to the coroner. He did not come because of the storm. Undertaker Ranck was sent for and he came out about eight o'clock this morning."

She continued, "We thought Garrity died of hemorrhage of the lungs. We had the undertaker remove the body at once."

They asked her if Garrity had been in a melancholy frame of mind lately. Lucy replied, "He had been away for about a week on a spree. He was a great drinker. He never came home drunk or drank any around here. He knew we wouldn't allow it. But he had been feeling unwell. He told Joseph that he intended to go to town with him tomorrow. He wanted to get some medicine for his stomach. Joseph had told him that was fine."

She paused and then blurted, "I never had anything to do with Garrity. I hardly ever spoke to him. Bill would sit on the porch sometimes. He was a man who said but little and I never talked with him much. I hope that, whatever you do put in the paper, you will not say that the man was murdered. I have been feeling just as nervous as I can be ever since this morning.

"The coroner came out here at noon. When the body was taken to the undertaker's they discovered the man had been shot. I couldn't believe it. He began to question me as though the man had been murdered in this house. He didn't get much out of me. We all believed this morning that the man died of hemorrhage of the lungs. I shall believe nothing else until I find differently."

The reporter then asked Lucy, "Was Garrity troubled with his lungs?"

Lucy took a deep breath, her fatigue showed all the more. "He was not. During the time I have known him he has never complained of illness. Only when he had been drinking and then he would be merely feeling unwell."

The artist from *The Gazette* was drawing a sketch of the house. After which he drew the floor plan of the second floor. The reporter continued to question Lucy about the events that led to this possible crime as the sketches were being done.

He asked her if there were any possibility for a person to get into the house through the windows and shoot Garrity in his bed.

"No, the windows upstairs are closed and fastened and there are screens on the outside. No one could get into the house that way."

Then the reporter asked whether anyone could have come into the house, possibly making his or her way to Garrity's room?

Lucy stated, "The doors are always left open. Whether anyone could have come in and gone upstairs without being heard I don't know."

Little Walter had been quietly listening from the front porch. The adults had nearly forgotten his presence until he piped up, "I didn't know anything about Bill being dead until I woke up this morning. I went to the barn with Pa and Bill last night after supper. I helped Bill feed the horses. Then we went to pump water for the stock. Bill and Pa and I stood at the pump talking for a while. When we got through pumping water I came to the house. I washed my face and feet then went upstairs. Bill was sitting at the table looking at the paper with Pa.

"After Bill died Pa came upstairs and took me out of bed. He carried me downstairs and put me in bed down here. I didn't wake up, didn't know where I was until I woke up this morning. But you ought to have seen Bill's bed this morning. His pillow was all covered with blood and the bed was soaked with blood. This morning Ira Conley and Otto found Otto's gun. It was hid in the oats bin. Otto purchased the gun in Chicago. It was always hanging over the bed in our room."

The newspapermen gathered all the information they needed, and took their leave, which made Lucy extremely glad. She was feeling exhausted and nervous, and Joseph, for some reason, had not returned home from his milk route.

# Chapter 6

Joseph had finished his last delivery of the day at the First Street Restaurant, near the old Arcade Hotel. His milk wagon was quite elaborate for the times, with the milk kept nice and cold in the summer, and in the winter kept from freezing with a small stove. Joseph had his team tied up with the milk wagon, and as he left the restaurant he noticed Mr. Donahue, a neighbor, had pulled his own wagon close to Joseph's. He walked over to his neighbor and climbed up on the wheel and began talking about Garrity dying.

Mr. Donahue had known Garrity too and he questioned Joseph. "Does Garrity have anything in wages coming to him?"

"No, he does not."

Mr. Donahue let Joseph know he had been talking with some of their other neighbors, and they had concluded that since Garrity had no money, they would raise enough to give him a decent burial.

This idea sounded good and proper to Joseph so he volunteered to donate five dollars. "I want to see Bill given a decent burial," he responded, "and I would like to arrange to attend his funeral."

Their conversation over, Joseph headed across the street, just as Marshal Kozlovsky approached him. The marshal told Joseph that he needed him to come to the station since he was under arrest.

"I supposed you want to ask me something about the young man who died at my house last night?" Joseph asked.

"Yes, what did he die of?" the marshal asked.

"Why, I don't know, hemorrhage I guess, I'm no doctor."

Later at the station, Joseph was questioned by County Attorney Mekota and Coroner King. As Joseph began his statement he was unaware that Otto had come to town to find him, and the reporters were questioning Lucy, who was wondering why he was not home. The same reporters met up with Otto and questioned him on his way back to the farm.

Joseph's statement began: "I was awakened in the night by a noise upstairs. I went up and called to Garrity but received no response. Going to his bedside I saw that he was dead. The condition of the body indicated that he had died from hemorrhage of the lungs. I have employed Garrity for some time and paid him good wages. Bill was well-liked by all the family. There has never been a quarrel between any of us. Garrity had come down to Cedar Rapids to the circus. He had taken to drinking and stayed longer than he expected. Bill returned home in the milk wagon with me on Monday."

Joseph continued. "Garrity worked about the place all day Tuesday. He retired about nine o'clock Tuesday night. He took a lighted lantern and a pitcher of water upstairs with him." Joseph then said he could assign no reason for the sudden attack that he claimed must have ended Garrity's life.

After another break he was interrogated by Deputy Marshal Brown, and was told he would have to give a plausible account of Garrity's death. Marshal Kozlovsky came into the room as well. By this time Joseph was exhausted, hungry and nervous. After a sleepless night, and a full day's work, on top of the emotional upheaval, he had nothing left. He admitted to the two officers that he killed Garrity but claimed he had acted in self-defense.

Joseph was allowed supper and a short break from interrogation after his confession while County Attorney Mekota and Coroner King were notified that Usher had made a partial confession. Joseph was cool and collected upon being brought into Deputy Marshal Brown's office, following his supper break. He was seated in a large and comfortable chair, not how you would picture the scene of a suspect being questioned. In the presence of officials, Dr. King, and C.K. Ranck, Joseph provided a detailed statement while a representative from the *Cedar Rapid's Gazette* took shorthand. Joseph was not subjected to any cross-examination; he reiterated his statements without any material change at any point.

Marshal Kozlovsky calmly began, "Now, Mr. Usher, if you want to make a statement under oath. This is Mr. King, the coroner, and Mr. Mekota, the County Attorney. The gentleman from *The* Gazette will take it down. You can tell it just as you told it to me."

"Don't I have the privilege of an attorney?" Joseph asked.

The marshal replied, "Yes, you can have an attorney if you want one. I would like you to tell the coroner exactly what you told me before supper."

Joseph intimated he was willing to make a statement. He rose and was sworn in by Coroner King.

Joseph's story was as follows. "Do you wish me to go in to details? Well, I will tell the exact truth.

"I had never had any trouble with Garrity, nor had any quarrel with him. I think he was out of his head when I went up the stairs. That's the reason he come at me. It was about nine o'clock, I guess. I heard a thumping noise upstairs. I went up to see what it was. When I got upstairs I turned towards the west window. I was raising it up to keep out the rain. It was when he jumped at me and says, 'I am going to kill you!' He was a big man and I am very weak.

"I grabbed that little rifle."

At this point Joseph was asked, "That was in your son's room, wasn't it?"

Joseph replied, "I don't recollect. I was so frightened I don't recollect. I think the gun was by the open window."

Then he was asked, "You picked up that rifle, then what did you do?

"I shot at him then. He said he was going to kill me and I shot him. He was between me and the stairs."

"Did he have anything in his hands?"

"I could not say."

"Was he on the floor?"

"He was standing on his feet on the floor."

"Was he in motion?"

"Yes, going right towards me."

"What did you say?"

"I did not say anything. I just grabbed up the gun and pointed it at him. It was the first thing I could get hold of."

"Was there a light in the room?"

"He had a lantern."

"Was the light burning?"

"Yes."

"After you pulled the trigger, then what did he do?"

"He fell right back on the bed. I presumed he was killed."

"Did he say anything?"

"No sir."

"Did you cover him up?"

"No, sir."

"What did you do then?"

"I was so nervous and frightened I don't know just what I did do then. I called the boy and sent him down to Spicer's."

Joseph paused. "I called my wife and son Otto."

Upon further examination he admitted that he had gone to the granary where he hid the rifle before alarming the household. "Garrity was such a strong man. He could easily have killed me if I had been defenseless."

Joseph was then asked if the rifle was not in his son's room. He replied, "I did not think it was," denying emphatically that he had first secured the gun in anticipation of trouble with Garrity.

When questioned concerning Garrity's position on the bed, Joseph sighed. "The man fell back on the bed after being shot. He only gasped once or twice. We never touched or moved the body until the undertaker arrived."

There was an effort to establish a possible motive for the

shooting. Joseph was asked if he had ever had any cause to be suspicious of Garrity–possibly due to attention the man had shown his wife.

He replied, "No I have not. I believe my wife to be a true, virtuous woman. She has never showed Garrity any favors other than any employee about the place would have received."

Joseph went on to admit, "I told the undertaker that Garrity had died from hemorrhage. I thought it would be better to make a complete statement. I expected the officials to make an investigation."

Joseph claimed, "Garrity had come to town on circus day. He had been on a bender and did not return home until last Monday evening. The fellow acted queerly, as he had at many other times. He kept a quantity of liquor by him nearly all the time. Bill had spells during which he did not act rational. I am convinced that Garrity was out of his mind Tuesday night. Else he would not have attempted to attack me, his friend and employer."

# Chapter 7

The charge before Joseph A. Usher is as follows: *State of Iowa vs. Joseph Usher, before J. F. Rail, Justice of the Peace of Rapids Township. Linn County, Iowa. The defendant is accused of the crime of murder. For that on or about the 26th day of May, 1903, at Clinton township, Linn County Iowa, the said defendant did feloniously, willfully, deliberately and premeditatedly and with malice aforethought, with a rifle loaded with powder and ball, which rifle was then and there held in the hands of said defendant, discharge the said ball from said rifle, upon and against the body of William Garrity inflicting a mortal wound thereby, of which wound the said William Garrity did then and there die.*

# Chapter 8

Lucy was extremely nervous after Otto left to find his father. She paced the wooden front porch, staring off into the distance, awaiting the return of her husband. Since Otto had taken her horse and buggy, she was stuck helplessly waiting. Her nerves had never felt so raw.

Lucy and Joseph had been having a rough time in their marriage. She had a great love for him, but her moods very often got the best of her and caused her to act in ways which she often came to regret. Joseph knew all too well how jealous Lucy could get over the slightest provocation, and he worried about his young wife's mental stress.

As Lucy paced and wrung her hands, Otto retraced his father's milk route. He knew the route by heart, so he began with the last customer, and found he did not have to go any further. At Joseph's last stop in front of the old Arcade Hotel, there stood their team and milk wagon, tied just as his father had left them. Otto could determine from the horses' footmarks in the dirt that they had been there for quite some time, and they were restless to return home to their barn for the night.

Joseph's son entered the sheriff's office with a sick feeling in his stomach, but he put on a brave face to discover his father's whereabouts. Otto was not pleased to find out that his father was being held for questioning, but at least he had an answer for Lucy and Walter, waiting back home. He felt odd leaving the Sheriff's office without his father returning to the farmhouse with him, but he knew he had to go, so he tied Lucy's horse and buggy behind the milk wagon and headed back.

The two reporters who had questioned Lucy were going in the opposite direction from Otto, heading back to the city. They halted the boy.

"Where is your father?" the reporter asked him.

"He is being held in town as a witness," he replied.

The reporter then asked what Otto knew about the affair at his house.

"Well mister, I don't know as I ought to say anything about this matter. There's to be a hearing and I don't believe I ought to say a word."

The reporter didn't take this as a deterrent. "Had Garrity complained of being tired of life?"

"He had not," Otto replied, "but Bill had been complaining about his stomach. He told father he was going to town with him tomorrow. He wanted to get some medicine." Otto paused and then declared, forgetting his thoughts about not speaking to the men, "I was asleep when father awakened me right away. Garrity was bleeding at the mouth. He lived not more than a minute after I saw him." Otto looked at the direction of home. "I do not care to say anything more on the subject. I have all the chores to do after I get home. I need to go," and then he drove on as the two reporters watched him disappear down the road.

# Chapter 9

The Ushers were fortunate to have good neighbors and friends help out. Mrs. Weed was worried about Lucy and the boys, so she stopped by the farmhouse that night and offered the three of them to spend the night. The Ushers gladly accepted the invitation. Without Joseph at home, and in light of what had transpired the night before, the Ushers were not too eager to be alone. Before they left for the Weeds' home, Otto had the help of Floyd Weed and another boy their age to get the evening milking chores done.

The next morning the Ushers went back to their farm and found a team of horses hitched to a surrey, standing at the hitching post. Presently two policemen came into view, giving Lucy quite a start. The officers explained they were there to bring the family to town. Warrants had been secured from Justice Rall after midnight, Wednesday, and about three o'clock Thursday morning, May 28, 1903. Night Captain McKernan and Officer Egey Meyer were the officers sent to the farm to arrest Mrs. Usher, Otto and Walter.

Floyd Weed had returned to help Otto get the morning chores done, and the policemen waited while they did their chores, and got the milk set to go for Harry Lensch, who knew Joseph's route and was willing to take over for the day. After chores, Lucy and the boys got changed into clean clothes and were ready to leave by eight o'clock in the morning.

Once the Ushers had arrived in town, Lucy was placed with the police Matron, while Walter and Otto were taken upstairs to a clean room in the women's department, which seemed to be empty. When Walter saw the iron door and locks he cried. The jailer felt sorry for the little boy so he let him go to his mother.

The Ushers were each questioned separately by Coroner King and the County Attorney Mekota who began with Otto's statement.

Otto stated: "I am the oldest son living at home. I turned sixteen years of age last November. I had been compelled to marry my stepmother's sister, Hulda, after she had been ruined. There was trouble between father and my stepmother because of this sister.

"In a round-about way, I understand why my stepmother blames father rather than myself. Since that time the woman has secured a decree of divorce from me.

"Ever since then there has been more or less friction between father and my stepmother. Both have been of a more hasty temper. Their quarrels usually began with hints or accusations of infidelity. Sometimes Lucy making accusations, sometimes father."

He continued. "My stepmother has been subject to frequent spells. The spells occur when Lucy's mind is unbalanced.

During these spells she makes accusations against father. It seems to be on her mind, but as a general thing, the couple seems to think a good deal of each other."

At this point, County Attorney Mekota ended the questioning of the boy. When Otto was dismissed, Coroner King called Lucy to make her statement. She was dressed becomingly in a brown skirt and white waist, accessorized by jewelry and a gold watch. Coroner King noted that Mrs. Usher was an attractive woman of medium size, with black hair, brown eyes and cheeks glowing with good health.

Mrs. Usher showed an evident desire to have the testimony over, and she spoke with a nervous directness. Frequently she repeated, "I have told you all I know and can tell you no more." She declared, "I have given my husband no cause for jealousy. I have never accepted any undue attentions from Garrity. I heard a slight noise. It was as if someone were saying 'Oh!' or 'Ouch.' I rushed upstairs as fast as I could. It seemed I only touched one step on the way up. Garrity was lying perfectly still making no sound. Joseph put his hand on Garrity's forehead. He said Garrity was dead."

At this time Coroner King excused Mrs. Usher, and upon reviewing his notes realized Otto had said he was there at the same time. 'There was a sound in Garrity's throat. It was between a gurgle and a rattle, which continued for a short time.' Usher himself stated that no one touched the body in any way; however, Otto stated that he bathed the dead man's forehead with water.

Mekota called Walter for his statement, the last Usher family member to give a testimony.

Walter said, "Father and Garrity had a long talk at the milk house. It was about something, but I do not know what it was. I have an idea that if father said he shot Bill, he did it." The child did not explain or tell how he came to such an idea.

Mekota excused little Walter so he and King could review the testimony. They found a strange part of the testimony was given by Otto who said on the fatal night Garrity had come into the kitchen, after the evening milking was done, where the boy sat reading. Garrity rested his hands on the table, looked straight at Otto and said, "Otto, do you think they would harm a man because of something he had said? I heard I had said something and I would get in trouble for it."

"Why no, Bill," returned Otto. "I don't see how they could harm you because of what you have said. I think you must be a little off," Otto declared.

This was all Otto said about the matter, and he knew no reason for Garrity having made such a statement.

As far as the rifle was concerned, in reviewing the testimonies, the two men found that Usher said he had picked up the gun from the room where Garrity slept. The two boys said the rifle hung over Otto's bed on a nail. In order to fetch the rifle, Usher would have had to pass through Garrity's room into the boys' room and return. Otto had testified that he had hunted with the rifle last Sunday, and he had taken out the loaded shell before hanging the rifle up again. The shells were loose in a large box that stood on the bureau.

Joseph's testimony stated he was closing the bedroom window, turned around and shot Garrity; however, Lucy stated she herself had closed the windows during the afternoon rainstorm, and they were not reopened. The questions were mounting: why did Joseph go to Garrity's room after the family was asleep? Why did Garrity take the lantern upstairs with him that night? Was Garrity asleep or awake when Usher killed him? Was this a deliberate, cold-blooded murder, or was this a murder done in a quarrel?

The statements by the Usher family had been completed as the day approached noon. Otto was brought dinner on a tray. The turmoil of the day did not affect his youthful appetite, so he cleaned his entire platter. Although Otto was mystified regarding the entire event, he seemed to have little fear, so after dinner he lay down on a pretty decent bed and fell asleep until an officer unlocked the door to fetch him.

Lucy, Otto and Walter were taken to the office of the Justice of the Peace to be arraigned. They each were reflecting upon the statements they had made that morning to the Coroner and to the County Attorney as they made the short walk up the street. While they sat and waited for their arraignment, Joseph was brought in by Deputy Marshall Brown.

This was the first time the family was reunited since Joseph had left the day before on his milk route. So much had transpired since he left for a seemingly normal day. Joseph stopped and kissed Lucy and nodded to his two boys.

Otto was taken into a room with his father and Mr. Redmond, the attorney the Ushers had hired.

"What is this all about?" Otto asked his father.

"I cannot explain right now," Joseph replied.

Mr. Redmond asked Otto a few questions. He said. "As of now I have not had time to review and plan a defense. Otto, when they put you on the stand at this time you are not to answer any questions on the grounds that it might lead to convict you."

Otto did as he was told although he did not agree that this seemed the right thing to do. Attorney John M. Redmond appeared for all the defendants as the preliminary hearing continued. In the case of Lucy and the boys the hearing was continued until five p.m. Thursday afternoon, after which time they were expected to be allowed to return home. In the case of Joseph, the hearing was continued until nine o'clock Friday morning, May 29, 1903. In addition, the defendants were all committed without bail until after their preliminary hearings.

# Chapter 10

O n Thursday, May 28, 1903, at two o'clock, the inquest commenced in the east side office of Undertaker Ranck, at Second Avenue and Fourth Street. Those who were called to be in the coroner's jury were H. B. Simpton, Joseph Stoddard, and John M. Terry. In addition to the Usher family, a number of neighbors were subpoenaed as witnesses.

The first witness called to the stand was Courtney Ranck, who testified: "I was called to the home of Joseph Usher at four-fifteen Wednesday morning by Lewis Werner. We went to the home of Usher. Mr. Werner said that the funeral would be held at Kenwood. I thought it would be better to bring the body back to the city for burial. Mr. Thomas Gibney met us when we drove into the Usher farmyard. Mr. Usher and his wife and two children were there.

I asked the Ushers, 'Was it a murder or a natural death?'

"'It was a natural death,' they said.

"I then asked, 'Did you call a doctor?' And the answer was 'no.'"

Mr. Ranck continued with his testimony. "Mr. Usher said the man had died about nine-thirty. He heard a slight noise and went upstairs. He found blood gushing from Garrity's nostrils. Mr. Werner believed Usher's story, and so did I.

"The Ushers said the coroner had been notified. He said he would be out the first thing tomorrow morning. We decided to take the body to the city. We went upstairs and found the body lying with feet to the east. His head was to the west. Straight up and down the bed with one foot braced against the footboard. The left arm lay over the stomach. The head was bent slightly to the left. The body lay on its back. The shirt and undershirt were both buttoned. It was a double bed and the body lay on the front side of it."

Mr. Ranck continued speaking. "Arriving at the morgue I began sponging the matted blood off the face. I unbuttoned the shirt and laid back the lapels of the shirt. I found the bullet wound.

"In the meantime Coroner King had come in. We both examined the wound, and came to the conclusion Garrity had been murdered.

"In my opinion Garrity could not have been shot as he lay in bed.

"Mr. Usher had spoken of going to one of the neighbors. He wanted me to wait till one of the neighbors came."

Coroner King then asked the witness, "Do you regard removing the body as complying with the law? You should have known not to remove the body before the arrival of the coroner."

Mr. Ranck replied, "In view of all the circumstances and what were the wishes of the dead man's relatives I think my actions were perfectly proper. I told the Ushers not to re-move any of the clothing or bedding. Not until the arrival of the coroner."

In taking off the shirt the witness did not see any gunpow-der burns.

George Spicer, the Usher's neighbor, was the second witness called. "I have lived near the Usher farm for fifty-three years. Tuesday night Otto Usher came down and said he guessed Mr. Garrity was dead. He thought it was from hemorrhage.

I did not go to the Usher farmhouse. But Mr. Usher was at my house twice. The first time was to borrow some kerosene.

I heard Mr. Usher ask Conley to go up and help. Otto need-ed help to burn up the furniture and bedding. Usher said the coroner had directed that they be burned up. Garrity and Usher appeared to be good friends."

Following Mr. Spicer's brief statement, Egbert Weed was called. Mr. Weed stated: "I have lived across the road from Mr. Usher for nineteen years. Otto Usher came to the house and said Garrity was dead. Then I went over to Ushers. I did not go up to see Garrity. I thought it better to wait till Gibney came."

When asked if he had ever heard that Mrs. Usher was jeal-ous of her husband, the witness took a long time to consider. Finally in a hesitating way, Mr. Weed said, "No, I had never heard that Usher was jealous of his wife."

Next Mr. Weed was asked if he had ever heard of the trouble between Otto Usher and Mrs. Usher's sister. Mr. Weed said: "I have heard talk that Mrs. Usher was jealous of her husband because of this. It was said that Mr. Usher's conduct toward Mrs. Usher's sister was not what it should have been."

It was general opinion of the neighborhood that Usher should have stood by the boy. He should not have allowed the marriage to take place. Even if a lawsuit followed. It was neighborhood talk that Usher was the father of his wife's sister's child. He made the boy marry the girl in order to shield his own wrong-doing.

Fred Lazell, city editor of *The Republican*, was called last. He testified, "I was one of those who heard Usher make his confession.

"At the police station Wednesday night Usher said that he was awakened by a noise that seemed like a thumping." He went on to repeat what Joseph had said in his confession.

Following this testimony, the inquest was completed for the day. The Usher family had been together in one room for the duration of the inquest—the two boys and Joseph and Lucy—and yet they never had felt so far apart. Joseph was exhausted and numb from the day's proceedings, as was his family. He was taken back to the city jail, while Lucy, Otto and Walter were allowed to leave. This was extremely difficult on the family, to see Joseph taken away once again. Lucy thought her husband appeared tired and sad, and his worn demeanor made her want to cry. She had begun this day with the confidence that all would work out for the best. Her neighbors and friends had been reassuring, and she pushed her fears aside to face the proceedings. Now, however, having heard the various testimonies in that office, she was terrified. Lucy had no idea what the future held for her family or for herself.

Perhaps what was most trying for Lucy was all that had come out in the testimony—all they had tried to keep quiet. The Usher's privacy was gone and this made her terribly upset in every way. Lucy had not recovered from her husband's infidelity with her sister, Hulda. How could she? Of course this incident had left her feeling insecure and jealous. Lucy's father had insisted that Hulda's reputation be salvaged or Joseph would have hell to pay, it was decided Otto would have to marry Hulda, since she would be ruined by the birth of a child out of wedlock. Joseph was against this marriage for obvious reason, and luckily for Otto the marriage was in name only, sine the two never went through with the plan—the boy was too young.

Emotionally exhausted the Ushers climbed up into their buggy to head back home to their farm, with Officer Egey Mayer, who had brought them in under arrest that morning, driving them away from the city, and away from their husband and father. Walter snuggled up beside Lucy where he felt safe, while Otto sat beside the officer, thinking about the chores he had to get done that evening with the help of his neighbor. Despite all the turmoil, work still had to be done. The Ushers had a long evening ahead—supper had to be made and the chores completed, just as if all were normal.

Little Walter fell asleep on Lucy's lap as soon as the town was behind them, and his closeness brought her the little bit of comfort it could afford. If only they could leave their troubles behind as easily as they left Cedar Rapids. Otto turned and saw his little brother sleeping soundly, lulled by the rhythm of the horse's feet on the dirt road. Lucy took in a deep breath and let out a sigh of relief as they neared the farm. The afternoon sun was settling in the sky, and the dimming light made their farmhouse look all the more inviting.

Otto felt a slight chill in the crystal clear air. Now the rain was gone, and the leaves of the trees and the grass all around them glowed in the dissipating light. Otto was tired from listening to the proceedings; he had wanted to testify, but Attorneys Redmond and Clemans would not allow him to testify against himself. Once again, Otto did not agree with what he was instructed to do by the lawyers, since their instruction went against his grain. He wanted to tell what he knew, and was frustrated by having to hold his tongue.

However, as they drove into the farmyard, Otto's mind turned to the chores that were awaiting him. The milking of cows needed to be tended to, and he had all the responsibilities that had once fallen to his father to keep up.

That evening the coroner's jury returned a verdict. They were called to investigate the manner in which William Garrity died, and their verdict was death as the result of being shot with a rifle by Joseph Usher. A great deal of testimony had been heard during the course of the day– which established the essential facts in the verdict. Yet, despite all the facts, a deep mystery remained, perhaps never to be resolved.

# Chapter 11

Late Thursday evening, May 28, Lucy at last was able to close the door to her bedroom. Relief washed over her; the end of the day had arrived and darkness surrounded their farmhouse. The boys had been more than helpful, filling in where their father could not, with the chores and the milking: the daily responsibilities they had learned so well. They, too, were exhausted, and after their supper was eaten, they dragged themselves off to bed. Walter looked to his big brother for male comfort in the absence of their father. For Lucy there was no one for such comfort.

Lucy placed her lantern down on the chestnut bureau and changed into her nightclothes. She pulled out the hairpins one by one that held her long black hair in place, brushed it smooth, and let it fall down her back. This was a sight that her husband loved at the end of the day. Tonight she did it for no one but herself.

When Lucy climbed between the cold sheets she felt the need to cry, but she knew once she began, she might not find the strength or reason to stop. The boys were certain to hear her sobs. There was so much to be saddened over; the grief of the very brutal week itself was more than most could bear. And when Lucy allowed herself to dwell upon the bitter memories of her sister, Hulda, and her affair with Joseph, it was more than her heart could fathom. The unwanted child born from their affair was a whole other sordid and disconcerting event. Her grieving was deepened by Otto being forced to marry her sister. Lucy felt sickened over a good young man like Otto being drawn into a situation he had nothing to do with. Why did this all have to happen? Lucy knew asking why never amounted to much. Now Bill was dead, and her beloved husband was in jail, charged with his murder. Lucy's body quivered under the heavy blankets; she could not get warm all by herself and a cold chill settled upon her with the darkness of night. The sobs came, uncontrollably, and she kept them muffled into her pillow so as not to alarm the poor boys. They had been through enough.

Lucy would have been disheartened to know that Joseph, too, was shaking. He was crying quietly in his prison cell. Joseph was a proud man of Native American descent and he could not abide by being imprisoned. There they were—a married couple, each crying quietly, neither one with anyone to provide comfort or solutions.

Friday morning came far too soon for Otto. He had to awake early to get the milking and chores done. He knew in order to attend his father's hearing, he needed to get the work completed. He wanted to face his father knowing he was not letting him down. The hearing was to begin by nine a.m.—which didn't give him much time.

When Otto came in from finishing chores, he found Lucy preparing breakfast for the boys. One look at her and he could see she'd been crying, and her nerves were causing her to shake. Even with a reddened face, she still appeared pale and tired from lack of sleep. Otto immediately became alarmed. He had the tendency to worry about others, and Lucy gave him great reason to worry.

Otto and Walter ate their breakfast in silence, while Lucy didn't eat a bite. They said their goodbyes and Otto took little Walter to the neighbors while he rode his horse to Reverend and Mrs. Lockwood's house. He hoped the Reverend and his wife could help his stepmother, so he told them of Lucy's condition, and did not hold back any of his concerns. One thing Otto didn't want was something to happen to Lucy while his father was in jail.

If anyone could help it would be the Lockwoods. Lucy had worked for them as a housekeeper before she married Joseph. In fact, Otto was pretty certain this was how his father had met Lucy, since the Lockwoods were on his delivery route. They were compassionate people and they agreed to ride out in the morning and check on Lucy. This comforted Otto and freed him up to ride into town for his father's hearing.

When Reverend and Mrs. Lockwood reached the Usher's farm, they found Lucy entirely distraught. Lucy smiled and wiped her tears upon opening the door; they had always been kind to her, and there was comfort in laying eyes upon other adults. Mrs. Lockwood decided immediately that Lucy needed to come home with them. There was no way she could leave her in such a state all alone.

Not much persuasion was needed to convince Lucy to leave the lonely farmhouse, and as soon as they settled at the Lockwood's she was persuaded to have a small bowl of soup and take an afternoon nap. Unfortunately, when Lucy awoke, her mental condition was worse. Neither food nor rest could soothe her.

# Chapter 12

Nothing of this magnitude had ever occurred in the southeastern part of Linn County. Of course there were the days of horse thieves and other such petty criminals being hunted down and even hung, but no event had caused this much talk and speculation prompted by the murder of William Garrity by dairyman, Joseph Usher.

Since this was such sensational and unusual news, talk of the murder spread like wild fire through the quiet county. Most people, like Lucy, were asking themselves why William Garrity was killed. Neighbors and friends of Joseph, people who believed they knew this hardworking man, were searching for a reason while they sat drinking and eating at the local pubs, and restaurants, or any other gathering place folks got together. Their conversations were spent mulling over the possible motives, and they discussed different theories regarding the events surrounding the murder. Over night the residents of Linn County had become detectives in their own right.

Joseph Usher was to be arraigned at nine o'clock the morning of Friday, May 29, 1903. The arraignment was in the court of Justice J.F. Rall on the charge of murder, and the expectation was the preliminary hearing would be waived. Joseph would then be held over for the Grand Jury, which met the following September, and as of yet, it was undetermined if he could be allowed to give bond.

J.F. Rall was the Justice of the Peace of Rapids Township, Linn County, Iowa, and he found the attorneys for Joseph Usher were not prepared. Consequently, they asked for a continuance, which was granted and set for Tuesday, June 2 at nine a.m. Attorneys Redmond and Clemens would decide whether they would request a preliminary hearing or waive it, turning Joseph over to the Grand Jury.

Not only did talk revolve around Garrity's murder, but the community began to examine Joseph Usher's life altogether. Of course, one thing that surfaced and did not reflect well upon Joseph, was the situation with Hulda, and speculation was that Joseph compelled his own son to marry his wife's sister. This was all hearsay, since no fact was known, but hearsay was all that was needed in such a time.

Upon further investigation into this unfortunate and sordid event in the Usher's family, Gills, Lucy and Hulda's father, was the one who insisted Otto marry his daughter. This speculation cast an entirely different light upon the development of the past few days in the once quiet county.

# Chapter 13

The wheels of justice were set in motion, and they moved along swiftly in this once serene Iowa community. Immediately after the continuance was granted, Attorney John M. Redmond, counsel for Joseph, applied to Coroner King for permission for both Dr. Skinner and Dr. Bender to examine Garrity's body. There were certain things that were necessary to prove, and the defense needed to establish the bullet's course. And so it was Coroner King granted his consent, and then informed undertaker Ranck of the need for autopsy.

Garrity's body was resting at the home of relatives on First Avenue, where his funeral was to be held. The doctors had no idea the difficulties that lay waiting for them, for Mr. Ranck refused to cooperate or comply, thereby stalling the examination from taking place. Even after the doctors explained they only needed ten minutes' to complete the examination, Mr. Ranck denied their request. This forced an appeal to County Attorney Mekota, who at once directed the undertaker to comply with Attorney Redmond's request.

However, Mr. Ranck, the ex-coroner, flatly refused to do so, claiming the relatives objected and the remains were interred at Kenwood cemetery.

Attorney Redmond was indignant, but King was even more so, since he had censured Mr. Ranck severely for his handling of the case from the very moment he had arrived at the Usher's home. Mr. King believed Mr. Ranck had years of experience as coroner, and he should have known it was improper and unlawful to remove, or even so much as touch the body without the coroner's permission. In addition, when Mr. Ranck was advised that Coroner King had been summoned, he paid no attention to this request. Mr. King's belief was that the undertaker had acted out of pure spite— his spite taking precedence over law. The undertaker suffered a chip on his shoulder; he felt he had not been treated fairly in the distribution of business doled out by Mr. King, whose brief and yet unfinished term had yielded much work that he had carried out with enthusiasm—despite insufficient remuneration. These are the politics that occur even in small communities.

Mr. King had no choice but to appeal for an order from the court–which would put Mr. Ranck in his proper place and keep him from interfering in any further proceeding with Garrity's case.

That morning in the courtroom, Otto was relieved to lay eyes on his father, if only for a brief time. There was comfort in being together, although they were not alone, and were under extreme and uncertain conditions. Joseph's son also felt proud, that he was upholding his end of things, managing the chores, keeping the routine of the milking running smoothly, and taking care of both little Walter and Lucy. He wished he could convey all this to his father with just a look, or the way he sat tall, not cowering and meek, but like the young man he was turning into more quickly than he ever thought possible.

The continuance was granted until the following Tuesday, June 2, and then Joseph was led back to the police station. Otto watched his father's shuffling walk, and thought he looked diminished and haggard, much like his stepmother. In just a short time, Lucy and Joseph had shown the results of the stress of this mysterious tragedy, and Otto worried what would happen as the time passed and the stress grew.

# Chapter 14

After the courtroom proceedings, Otto needed to return home to the farm. Lucy was foremost on his mind, and he wanted to check on her emotional state. He arrived to an empty house, and at first felt a sense of panic, but then remembered Reverend and Mrs. Lockwood had agreed to check on his stepmother. He knew they had taken Lucy home with them, and that she was in safe and capable hands, and for this he was relieved. Little Walter was the next concern Otto had, so he got on his horse and rode to the Weed's farm to see how his brother was faring. Walter was happy with a big plate of sugar cookies and the company of Mrs. Weed. Otto was entirely grateful for the help and support of their neighbors.

Floyd Weed accompanied Otto back to the Usher's for the evening chores and milking. The two handled things with competence and efficiency, and Otto knew if his father could see, he would be very proud. That night Otto returned to spend the night at the Weed's with his little brother. Being part of a family was far better than being alone in the Usher's empty farmhouse. There was a sense of normalcy in the routine of family life that both boys missed.

After a very long Friday night, the morning of May 30th at last arrived, and with the light of day came the realization that Lucy needed more help than the Reverend and his wife could provide. They drove Lucy in their buggy to Cedar Rapids, after preparing for the day, and arrived at St. Luke's Hospital, where Lucy was admitted, having suffered from nervous prostration. No one yet knew how long she would be in the hospital–the concern being only that she got rest and recovered.

Lucy was quiet. She had given into the state that had overtaken her, and no longer worried about her duties back at the farm. All she felt was the enormity of all that had transpired, and she could not crawl out from under it no matter how hard she tried. The Reverend and Mrs. Lockwood left Lucy with her over night bag and a hug. They knew she was in competent hands and the hospital staff would tend to her needs. She had been unfortunately transformed from the confident young woman who had arrived to work at their home not so very long ago, and now they only wanted her to get better.

# Chapter 15

On Tuesday morning, June 2, 1903, in the presence of scores of spectators Joseph Usher was taken to the courtroom of Justice J.F. Rall. Just after nine o'clock the Justice called the hearing to order and Joseph Usher was to answer to the charge of murder. Many of the Usher's neighbors, as well as residents from further away in the county, were present. There was a longing for an answer, and a curiosity that was fed by the mystery of a murder– something that just didn't happen there.

Captain Kroulik brought in the prisoner, who was securely handcuffed: an odd sight for a dairyman to be paraded like some sort of social deviant. The crowd stared steadily at the man accused of deliberately taking the life of William Garrity. Defensively, Joseph kept his eyes down, looking at no one when he entered. He exuded shame. A proud man such as himself, under these sensational circumstances, was absurd.

Joseph took his seat at the end of the table, and made one hurried glance at those assembled as well as the witnesses who had been summoned. Then he lowered his tired eyes and tried to give the gawking audience no further attention. Only when his attorneys, Redmond and Clemens, entered, did Joseph lift his stare from the wooden table.

County Attorney Mekota appeared as well, and there was a brief consultation. He announced the attorneys for the defense were not ready. More time was needed to prepare for the preliminary hearing. The lawyers asked for a further continuance until Friday, and Justice Rall granted them their request until Friday afternoon at one o'clock. Attorney Mekota asked the attorneys for the defense to state whether or not they would waive the preliminary hearing or have the state's witnesses in attendance.

To this Mr. Redmond stated, "At this time we are not prepared to say. We have not decided whether we shall demand a preliminary hearing or we shall waive. Here is a man charged with a grave crime. He has heretofore borne a splendid reputation. He is on the shady side of life. Up to this time his reputation has been good in every respect. He has the respect and esteem of his neighbors. His life has been in every way worthy. It is true that some tongues are wagging now that he is under arrest. Their comments on this charge count for little.

There is a deep mystery about this affair, which the state cannot understand. Perhaps we do not yet fully comprehend. I may say at this time it is our intention to demand a preliminary hearing. It may be that the light we expect to get on the case will change. Possibly we shall not feel called upon to demand a hearing but shall waive. In that case we will notify the county attorney by Thursday night, so he can tell the state's witnesses they need not be present."

The short time that Attorney Redmond had the floor, the crowd listened intently as did Joseph who had a stolid look upon his face, evidently deep in meditation. Occasionally his brown eyes flashed as he made a sweeping glance at those assembled. There were faces he clearly recognized, but now they may as well be strangers, not acquaintances, not neighbors nor friends he had been rubbing shoulders with for years—socializing and carrying out his honest business of milk delivery. By the look on his face, it was apparent that Joseph understood all too well the gravity of his crime.

Of course the relatives of William Garrity were present. They were a formidable and solemn bunch–Thomas Gibney, a cousin, Peter Garrity, from Sioux County– his full brother. C.H. Melons, a half-brother from Omaha was there too, and the family let it be known the case would be prosecuted for all it was worth. They were determined to unearth, if possible, whatever mystery was connected to the death of their relative.

Otto was present through out the proceeding without his stepmother by his side. He sat bravely, his one desire to appear strong for his father. Some of the Usher family had arrived in town that morning, and although they were not present in the courtroom, just knowing they were nearby was consoling for Otto. He couldn't help but grimace when the handcuffs were placed once again on his father's wrists before he was taken from the court back to his cramped cell at the police station. Joseph was followed by the coroner, and Otto thought his father appeared frail for the first time in his life.

Tuesday afternoon Otto and two of his relatives were admitted to the jail where they found Joseph locked in one of the inner steel cells. They were admitted to the corridor that was itself surrounded by steel bars, outside of which was another corridor and then the brick walls of the jail. This was obviously the first time Otto had been inside a jail, and the sight of it unsettled his young spirit. His father peered out through the bars at his family. His face haggard and his week's growth of black beard gave him an unfamiliar and somewhat wild appearance. Joseph seemed older in the semi-darkness of his inner cell, as if much more time had transpired than a mere week.

"I hope everything will come out all right," he spoke in a quiet tone of voice that was not typical for him. He broke into a half sob, and spoke with kindness and guidance to his son, as to how to proceed with the farm work. He bade him go and visit his stepmother and soothe her with kindness as well. There was a clear and pained concern on Joseph's face.

Otto and his relatives felt sorry for Joseph, a man who had always worked hard, putting in long days, never sparing himself for the well-being of his family. He was not a shirker. He was faithful to his patrons, no matter what ailments may have plagued him or how severe the weather had been in the Iowa countryside. He toiled fifteen, sixteen, sometimes eighteen hours a day for years on end. Due to his hard work he had accumulated a large property, and he realized it was too much to maintain. He would be unable to continue his dairy business; even if he should be acquitted, he knew selling was inevitable.

This thought was humbling and sad. All his toil and self-denial now counted for nothing. The paltry accumulations, the fruit of so much effort, would be wiped out—all the result of the black crime he confesses he committed. He had confessed to have taking the life of his fellowman. How could he even ask for or expect any semblance of sympathy. Joseph has given up all hopes of his life, his farm, his livelihood. Just as Lucy had fallen into despondency, so had her husband.

# Chapter 16

The daily paper reported a bill of sale from Joseph Usher to John M. Redmond for thirty cows, milk cans, as well as the milk route and such for six hundred dollars. The transfer of the Usher's one hundred-acre farm to John M. Redmond was also noted, with the property being given value of six thousand dollars. The article read as follows: "Joseph A. Usher, to John M. Redmond, warranty deed 20 lic and n 1-2 ne sc. 26 and nw. nw. 27 all 53-3 (subj. nlg. $6,000)."

As of this date the defense had yet to make application for the examination of the body of Garrity. As if tongues had not been wagging enough up to now, they were wagging all the more that morning as rumor gained currency that Otto had made a confession. Joseph's son admitted that he, alone, was responsible for the death of Garrity.

Isaac Usher, a half-brother of Joseph's, traveled down from South Dakota, accompanied by his oldest son who was, himself, engaged in farming. Apparently Isaac Usher had a conversation with Otto in which the statement was made that he had killed Garrity—not his father.

# Accountable: The Joseph Usher Story

Coroner King and County Attorney Mekota searched for Isaac Usher that morning to discuss this recent rumor. When they recounted the supposed confession, Isaac flatly denied having made any such statement about Otto, even though it had come from good authority that Isaac had told a local farmer. This farmer lived no more than two or three miles from the city, and said Otto had confessed to Isaac that he had done the killing. The farmer to whom Isaac made the statement did not believe he had dreamt the conversation up, but perhaps Isaac just didn't have a clear understanding of what he was discussing at the time. For Isaac to make such a statement, if it were not the truth, seemed entirely strange. But there was a lot about the Garrity case that was strange and seemingly unknowable.

Many people had come to believe that Garrity was not murdered in his bed, but was instead killed in the kitchen on that fatal night. The presumption was that his body was then carried upstairs by Joseph, and placed upon the bed. However, there were so many strange circumstances in connection with this murder, all those who waited for clarity were hopeful that in the next few months the mystery would be unraveled.

The day before the hearing, Thursday, June 4, all anyone could talk about was Garrity's murder. The plea of insanity would be offered in defense of Joseph Usher. The motive for the crime may have been that Garrity threatened Joseph, perhaps in divulging scandalous information related to Otto's marriage to Hulda.

Joseph's attorney stated that morning that he did not believe his client would kill a chicken, let alone murder another person. Perhaps Joseph may have fired the shot that killed Garrity, but he didn't believe there was anything exhibited in Joseph's nature to willingly kill anyone. Attorney Redmond remarked, "Joseph is naturally a very nervous man. He has lived there in the vicinity of his home for the past fifty-three years. There is not a neighbor to be found that will say that he ever had a quarrel with any man." The attorney admitted he thought Joseph may be a little off, but so far as being able to transact business he had shown excellent judgment in his interactions with all the people with whom he ever had any dealings. "With all the information that I have been able to get about this man," said Mr. Redmond, "I believe Joseph is more to be pitted than censured."

Attorney Redmond hoped to unearth more facts about his client's case before the hearing. There were a number of mysterious circumstances connected with the case at the beginning. When asked, the attorney denied Otto refusing to sleep at home. He said with the exception of two nights, Otto was staying at the house. His Uncle Isaac then came to stay with him.

Joseph's attorneys didn't have much else to say. Evidently they were putting great efforts into probing to the bottom of their client's case. From the little Attorney Redmond had offered, there was every reason to believe the defense was preparing for one of the greatest defenses made for any single person in Linn County who had been charged with the crime of murder.

Otto was exhausted, and was so grateful that his Uncle Isaac and his son had come to support them. They were there to lean on emotionally, and to lend a hand with all the difficult labor. The corn was in need of being planted, but first the soil had to be plowed, and additionally, forty acres needed to be worked. The weather had finally cleared, and with the dryer soil, the acres were ready for plowing. Otto could not do all this work alone, as well as preparing himself to be called as a witness at the preliminary hearing the next day.

# Chapter 17

Joseph was not able to sleep much, and Friday morning, June 5, came after a restless night. The jail matron brought his breakfast of toast, scrambled eggs and hot coffee, but along with a good night's sleep went Joseph's appetite. For one thing, he was leading a life he was unaccustomed to, with no physical exertion, and for another—he was emotionally raw and this dampened his hunger. He missed sitting down in his farmhouse for a good hot meal with Lucy and the boys. On this particular morning, he choked down very little of his breakfast.

The day before Attorney Redmond had brought Joseph a new brown suit, which he was expected to wear at the hearing that day. Otto visited with his father's razor in hand so Joseph could clean himself up and look presentable. This was the very furthest thing on Joseph's mind.

He had not seen his reflection in the mirror, and when he stood before the glass to shave, he was shocked by his appearance, which was pale and haggard. From the way his clothes were fitting, he could tell he had grown thin since he was placed under arrest, but his reflection drove his assumptions home. No wonder his family had such pained expressions when they caught sight of him.

County Attorney Mekota and his team had spent that Friday morning preparing. The state had made a strong case against Joseph Usher, and they were ready to present their case at the hearing–slated to begin at one in the afternoon.

Otto thought time flew that morning as everyone helped with the chores, and he forced himself to hurry, even to the point of being hasty, just so he could be done. He had been summoned to the hearing that day. His Uncle Isaac hitched the horse to the buggy and they left for town none to soon. Little Walter was left once again with the neighbors, while Otto's cousin remained at the farm to continue plowing. Otto was appreciative of his Uncle's presence at the hearing, and he knew his father would be comforted by his being there too.

On their way to the hearing Otto couldn't help but wonder how Lucy was doing at St. Luke's Hospital. Reverend Lockwood and his wife had taken his stepmother there nearly one week ago. Otherwise Lucy would have also been expected to testify at the hearing that day, instead she was admitted to the hospital with nervous distress. Otto tried to clear his head over his worry for Lucy. Right now the most pressing thing was his father's hearing and how he would fare.

When Otto and his Uncle Isaac made it to town they were on the early side, as it was just a little after twelve. Their mood was somber as they stabled the horse and walked over to Justice Rall's courtroom. Otto remembered what it had felt like to come to town with his father just last month, and not have a sense of shame of being scrutinized as he walked these very same streets and greeted the very same people. He was beginning to learn, at such a young age, how life could change on a dime.

The interest in the Garrity murder case had not simmered down; spectators thronged the office of the Justice—no one wanted to miss the preliminary hearing of Joseph Usher. There was scarcely enough space in the courtroom for the attorneys and the witnesses summoned, and the overcrowding made poor Otto feel claustrophobic. He was accustomed to open space and livestock, not hoards of people eager to learn his father's fate.

When Joseph was brought into the courtroom shortly after one o'clock, the spectators were stunned by his altered appearance, especially with Officers Kroulik and McGuire by his side, making Joseph seem even more vulnerable. As he took his place at the table next to his counsel, he riveted his eyes down once more as if the grain of the wood was of more interest than the proceedings that concerned him. At no time did he raise his head, or glance at a witness called, or even so much as take in a view of his surroundings.

Otto could not take his own eyes off his diminished father, and he felt an overwhelming sorrow for his condition. His Uncle Isaac was equally pained by his brother's plight, and he was disbelieving of the entire event although he knew, as sure as day, that he was sitting beside his nephew in this courtroom watching Justice Rall call the hearing to order with a swift hit of his mallet. All at once there was silence.

Mekota stood and began to call his first witness for the State, Ira Conley, who was a hired man on the Spicer farm.

The Spicer's place was only a quarter of a mile from the Usher's. Mr. Conley, when called, told essentially the same story he had narrated at the coroner's inquest.

"I was called to the Usher house shortly after Garrity died. I remained there until one o'clock in the morning." He explained about helping Otto clean out Garrity's room. "The stuff in the room including the bedding and bedstead were carried across the road. Everything was burned up."

Ira Conley winced as he described the bloody condition of the bed, and the position in which Garrity's body lay at the time.

"I have known Joseph for several years. Looking back, he appeared very nervous that night. He has been a very nervous man every since I have known him."

Conley continued, "I found the gun in the oats bin at the time the coroner instituted the search for it."

He answered the questions put to him very readily. He stated that he knew Otto had a gun, but he was unable to identify the weapon as Otto's. On cross-examination, Conley stated he had known Garrity for six or seven years. He described the man as being five-foot-six or seven inches in height.

Defense Attorney Redmond asked Conley numerous questions about Otto's rifle and the cartridges belonging to it. "On the Sunday before the shooting," Conley said, "I was at the Usher house and I was in Otto's room." He then described the room as well as where the gun and the bag of cartridges were kept.

Upon closer questioning, relating to the oats bin, the place where the rifle was found, Conley said, "The gun lay in the bin. It was on the floor and was partly covered with oats. There were no more oats in the bin than could be scraped up with a shovel. These oats lay between the cleats of the box. It looked as though the rifle had been shoved down in the oats. Or possibly the oats had been tossed around it after the rifle was placed in the oats bin."

Conley described the cartridges in Otto's bedroom as being about two feet from his bed, lying on the dresser.

When the questioning was over, he stepped down, and felt relief wash over him. This was nothing he had ever thought of himself having to do, and he was glad that his testimony had not revealed anything of a startling nature.

The second witness called was Egbert Weed, and he found himself equally nervous to testify as he stepped up in front of the crowd. Weed declared, "I am one of the oldest farmers in Clinton township and one of Joseph's near neighbors. I have made my home just across the road from the Usher place. I have farmed there for nearly fifty years."

Weed stated, "I was called to the Usher house on the night of the murder. I was led to believe from what Joseph and his wife had told me that Garrity's death was due to hemorrhage of the lungs. I was under that impression until I heard otherwise that Undertaker Ranck and the coroner had discovered that Garrity had been shot." After this statement, Weed was excused, and again, his testimony was essentially the same he had given before the coroner's jury.

After about a dozen witnesses had been summoned by both sides, the court was set to adjourn for the afternoon. Otto took in a deep sigh of relief since his testimony would not be taken until the next morning, when the hearing would continue. As his father was led back to his jail cell, Otto felt sadly frustrated. Not being able to discuss any of the court-room events with his stepmother or his father made it all feel that much more dire.

Otto and his Uncle Isaac excused themselves as soon as Joseph was gone; they could feel all eyes were on them— friends, neighbors, spectators as well as the Garrity family— all curious. This curiosity led to scrutinizing the actions of the Ushers. There was great admiration for Otto and how dedicated he was to his father, as well as his maturity and the handling of the farm's business, and his ability to tend to little Walter.

Otto and Uncle Isaac hitched the horse back to the buggy and headed west out of town, back to the farm and away from the harsh public eye. Arrangements were being made by Attorney Redmond to sell the dairy business, but until this happened, chores had to be done. Uncle Isaac could sense the nervous energy from Otto. He felt for the boy who was tired, and scared for his father's health, Lucy's health, and the family's uncertain future. Isaac knew that less than twelve days ago his brother's family was leading a normal life, at least that was how it had appeared. Hopefully on the way back to the farm, Otto would shed some light on the events that had so tragically changed the course of all their lives.

# Chapter 18

On Saturday, the sixth of June, Joseph Usher was brought to the hearing early. Justice Rall had called the hearing to order at nine a.m. sharp, and used his mallet to once again quiet the smaller crowd who sat in attendance.

Joseph seemed even more worn. There was deep worry on his brow that no previous hardship of life had ever caused. Perhaps today Joseph was troubled by his son having to testify. No father is eager to witness his own flesh and blood interrogated in a courtroom, standing before an eager audience.

County Attorney Mekota had been reviewing his documents from the day before; he noted that the coroner had been telephoned after Garrity's death. This bit of information was learned at the request of Joseph Usher, who had not been anxious to have Garrity's body removed from his farm.

Attorney Mekota put his notes down in a neat stack and stood, calling the first witness—Otto Usher—for the state. Joseph's son rose slowly and walked to the stand. Anyone who knew Otto recognized his gait was not his usual carefree step. Anyone watching, even those who already had their minds made up about guilt and about innocence, felt a sense of sorrow for Joseph Usher's son.

Otto stated, "I am sixteen years of age past and I have known Garrity in my lifetime. He has worked for my father since the middle of March. He worked about the house. He milked cows, hauled manure and did general work about the place." Even though Otto had been nervous, there was almost a sense of relief about him once he took the stand. Sometimes the anticipation is worse than the actual event, and Otto was settling down into answering the questions put to him. His shoulders relaxed, and his eyes had no trouble meeting the attorney's.

Otto told the attorney, "I saw Garrity on Monday in the forenoon, about eleven o'clock. It was Monday, the day before the night of the murder, and again Monday in the afternoon. Father had brought Bill back home later Monday after he finished the milk route."

He took a deep breath. "I went to town Tuesday to sell hogs and returned home in the evening around seven p.m. I ate supper with the rest of the family, including Garrity. After supper we finished the chores. Later I went to the house. I left father and Garrity talking at the pump near the barn. Finally father came into the house and sat down in the kitchen. He began looking at the paper. Garrity came in the kitchen shortly afterward. Father was tired and went to bed. Garrity sat part of the time in the sitting room. Garrity retired first. But before doing so he walked over to me and placed his hands on my chair saying, 'Otto, could they hang a man, or do anything with him, for saying something that he knew about another man?' I replied, 'I guess not Bill.' Soon after Bill went upstairs to bed."

Mekota asked Otto, "What took place next?"

Otto replied, "Father called me at half past nine or ten that night into Garrity's room.

I saw that Garrity was dying. There appeared to be but little life in him. Father was busily engaged in rubbing and bathing Garrity's feet. He was trying to resuscitate him. A moment later, I ran down to Spicer's. I was to inform the Spicer's and telephone to Garrity's cousin at Covington."

The County Attorney then asked the witness to identify the rifle, which Otto did, telling where Conley had found the weapon.

Otto testified, "I never kept my gun loaded when I had it in my room. Mr. King took the gun with him to town."

At this point it was approximately ten a.m. and Mekota announced he had no further questions for the witness.

Attorney Redmond stood on cross-examination, and Otto adjusted himself in the wooden chair. "When did Garrity step over to your chair? And when did he make the remark he had testified to?"

"It was shortly before nine," Otto replied. He was surprised and relieved to find out there were no further questions at this time. Otto was excused. When he left the stand, Joseph watched his son and felt he had become more of a man in the short time he was in jail than he ever believed possible. Father and son made eye contact, and without having to utter a word there was instant understanding between them. For the most part, these days, an exchange like this was the most communication they had.

Joseph shifted in his chair as the second witness of the day was called. If anyone could see his hands beneath the wooden table they would find them clamped down on either arm of his chair, bloodless and tense.

W.E. Holmes, city editor of *The Gazette*, was sworn in next.

Mekota began the questioning for the state. Mr. Holmes testified to being in the office of Marshal Kozlovsky the evening Usher made his confessions.

Mr. Holmes repeated, briefly, the details, with Joseph claiming he went to close the window and shooting Garrity in self-defense.

Mr. Holmes told who was present when Usher made his confession, and said, "I took a shorthand report of what Usher said and transcribed it." At this point Redmond rose and requested a copy of the transcript; however, Mekota objected.

The objection was overruled; therefore the transcript was subsequently presented. The two attorneys discussed the rights of the defendant's attorney to cross-question the witness, relative to what had been noted in the transcription. The attorney for the defendant admitted that it was the best evidence, and the court then allowed Redmond to proceed.

He claimed he wanted to test the witness's recollection to see how it compared with the transcribed statements. "Mr. Holmes, did Usher say something that evening at the time he was asked to make a statement? Did Usher ask if he did not have the right to have an attorney?"

The witness answered, "Yes, Usher did make such an inquiry."

The defense stated they would more than likely introduce some of the transcript in evidence. Later they would read that evidence. The attorneys had no more questions for Mr. Holmes at this time; he was excused.

There was a lull for a moment after which Justice Rall called for a brief recess, and Mr. Holmes left the courtroom. After the editor had gone, Redmond realized Holmes was required to answer a few more questions, so they called him back to the stand. Redmond once again stood before the witness and asked, "How long was Joseph Usher in the presence of those persons to whom he made the statements in his confession?"

The witness replied, "I think it was about half an hour. I did not take down everything that Usher said. I took down all that pertained to the case. Mr. Ranck asked Usher a few questions that evening about the removal of the body. I had not taken those remarks down. Usher made the statements about half past eight-o'clock that night. I took down all that Usher said. Everything was written down except the replies to half a dozen of the questions. They did not pertain directly to the case. When Usher was taken from the room, it was in the custody of one of the officers."

After Mr. Holmes' testimony was complete, Coroner King was sworn in at eleven a.m. He testified, "I have known Joseph Usher by sight for a number of years. I received a telephone message from Mr. Gibney at Covington. I was called to go to Usher's place. It was about one o'clock on the night of the murder. Because of the storm raging at the time I did not start out until morning. Wednesday morning I was within a quarter mile of the Usher farm when I met Undertaker Ranck bringing in the body. At this point I also met Thomas Gibney, Mr. Warner and Usher."

King continued by relating the story he had given at the inquest about discovering the bullet hole in Garrity's chest. "I immediately telephoned to Mr. Gibney. I asked him to meet me at Spicer's place. I told him a bullet wound had been found on Garrity. Mr. Gibney met me at the appointed place. From there we proceeded to Usher's. Usher was not there, but Mrs. Usher was. I told her that Garrity had been shot. I asked Mrs. Usher for the revolver. She said there was not any in the house. I started the search that was made for a gun on the premises. Conley was assisting in the search and found the rifle in the oats bin. I looked through the debris where the contents of Garrity's room were burned. I was hoping to find a firearm in it. The next time I saw Usher was in the city marshal's office. That is where I heard Usher's statement."

The Coroner paused and looked around the courtroom. For a time, while recounting his testimony, he had forgotten where he was. King had become lost in the details of the case, but now glanced around at all the familiar faces of the community staring back at him. He repeated the details of Usher's confession.

At this time, Coroner King was questioned about the conversation between himself, Usher, Gibney and Warner that had taken place near the Spicer's home. "Mr. Gibney was on a horse," he replied. "Usher had stated that Garrity was a hard drinker. Either Mr. Gibney or Mr. Warner remarked that they preferred Garrity's habit in this regard should not be made public. It was half past eight o'clock when I met Undertaker Ranck, Gibney, Warner and Usher near Spicer's." Mr. King described having found the cartridges on the bureau in Otto's room. In addition, he recounted the appearance of both Otto's room and the room Garrity had occupied. A number of questions were put to the witness but nothing new developed in his testimony than what had been already brought out at the inquest. There were no more questions, and Mekota dismissed him.

Justice Rall dismissed the court until one-thirty for dinner.

Although there may have been some hungry people in that courtroom, Otto and his father had no appetites to speak of; in fact, they each only had a shared hunger to see this day come to an end. The afternoon session came soon enough, after an opportunity for everyone to fill their stomachs and clear their heads. Mekota summoned Otto back to the stand and reminded him that he was still under oath. He began by asking, "What happened to the window in Garrity's room?"

Otto stated, "It was removed in the morning. When the body was taken from the room we wanted to get the bedstead out. It was taken apart."

Otto told the Attorney he had suggested to his father that the Coroner be called. Otto was told to step down as there were no more questions at this time.

The next witness called by the State and sworn in was Dr. W. S. King who had made the postmortem examination of Garrity's body. The doctor was asked to describe the bullet hole in Garrity's breast, the direction the bullet had taken, and the point at which it lodged in his back. Dr. King's testimony was essentially the same as he had given before. He testified to being present at the police station, when Joseph Usher made his confession. At this point, Mekota dismissed Dr. King.

# Accountable: The Joseph Usher Story

The city editor of *The Republican,* Fred J. Lazell, was the next witness Mekota called to the stand. He testified to being present at the police station when Joseph had made his statement. The editor stated, "I have known Joseph for a few years. Joseph made a statement in the afternoon before supper at the station. When he made his second statement, confessing to having killed Garrity, those present were Marshal Kozlovsky, Deputy Brown, the County Attorney, Coroner King, Messrs, McKernan, Ranck, Holmes and myself." Then he repeated the details once more. Usher said he heard a slight noise. That is what induced him to go upstairs that night. He thought one of his boys was sick. He had retired before he heard the noise. I asked him if he was dressed when he went upstairs and if he was dressed when he took the rifle to the oats bin. Joseph said, 'I don't think I was.' He stated that on going upstairs Garrity threatened to kill him. He took down the rifle and shot him."

At this point there were no more questions for Mr. Lazell and he stepped down. Mekota sat down as Defense Attorney Redmond stood and recalled Mr. Ranck to the stand. He was asked to give his version of Joseph's statement. "Joseph told that evening that he heard a noise upstairs. He went to Garrity's room to lower a window. When he got into the room Usher said Garrity got up on his feet. He started to come at him. He was threatening to kill him. Joseph grabbed the rifle from the wall and shot him. Joseph then took the rifle to the oat bin and hid it. He came back to the house and roused his family. Joseph had made a remark. He said that Garrity had been drinking hard. When he was drinking he didn't act right."

Defense Attorney Redmond then excused Mr. Ranck and recalled Otto to the stand once again. Each time Otto was called back, it got a little more familiar and a little easier. Talking in front of a courtroom of people was not enjoyable, but just like any unpleasant chore, Otto knew it had to be done. This time he was asked to tell when his family had gone to bed on Tuesday evening, the night of the murder. Otto stated, "My little brother went to bed first that night, then Garrity, and a short time after, I did. I don't know what time Lucy retired."

Redmond had no more questions for Otto, and the boy was all too relieved to remove himself from the stand. Once more he and his father locked eyes. Otto wished there was something he could do to remove the trouble from his father's face.

He sat down and watched as Redmond called Marshal Kozlovsky to be sworn in. The Marshal was then asked by the defense what he knew of the case, and he testified that Joseph Usher had made a statement to him confessing that he killed Garrity. The officer was cross-examined at length, but little additional information was brought out from what had been already been presented. The testimony was concluded for the afternoon, and Joseph Usher took in a deep breath with the knowledge he had made it through one more grueling day.

# Chapter 19

Late on the afternoon of June 6, 1903, the weather turned cooler and there were threatening storms in the area. The threat of bad weather had kept some of the locals from attending the day's hearing, and this gave Joseph slight comfort. The fewer eyes upon him the better, and especially when he felt the stares were judgmental, not concerned. Joseph was exhausted from the proceedings of the past two days. Oddly enough, he thought with relief of leaving the courtroom and having some privacy in his jail cell. He could not wait for this day to be finished.

Otto watched his father but could not discern where his mind or thoughts were, except that he seemed especially focused, and there was no doubt that Joseph had taken in every last thing that was said at the hearing.

A loud crack of lightening, followed by thunder, broke the silence in the still courtroom. The rain had begun again, just as the attorneys were to give their closing statements. Attorney Mekota stood to give his brief speech. He graphically presented the state's case.

"I have pointed out that the state has two strong lines of evidence. They are independent yet agreeing with each other in every particular. One of them is the confession of Usher himself. The second is the chain of circumstantial evidence that has been woven by the state. It is complete in every link. It is entirely independent of the statement made by Usher. And it's agreeing with it in every particular. The particulars are the storm, the time, and the rifle shot. Usher's notifying of the neighbors, the hiding of the rifle and Garrity's clothes that had been burned. In all these points the confession of Usher and the independent chain of evidence woven by the state are identical."

County Attorney Mekota closed by saying, "Everything points convincingly to Joseph Usher.He is the murderer of William Garrity." At this point, Mekota took his seat.

Defense Attorney Redmond stood for his closing statement. He, obviously, took a very different view. "Every scrap of evidence which the state has presented was obtained in the confession of Usher himself. It was Usher who had said he shot Garrity with a rifle. But, Usher's confession is a two-edged confession. He stated that he killed Garrity, however he also stated that he did it in self-defense. If his statement that he killed Garrity was to be creditable, then his other statement that he did it in self-defense should receive equal credit."

At this time Redmond proceeded to state all the points of the evidence. "These are points in Joseph's favor. The first being his actual nervousness. The fact he asked Spicer to let Thomas Gibney, cousin of Garrity, call the coroner. His running from the house dressed in his night-clothes.

And the fact that Joseph threw the gun behind the granary door."

Redmond continued with passion, "The testimony in Joseph's confession was that Garrity ate little supper that night. And then there was the strange question he asked Otto just before he retired. Garrity took the lantern to bed. It all added weight to Joseph's story. When Joseph went to Garrity's room after hearing a slight noise Garrity sprang up in bed and threatened to kill him. Joseph found the gun there, and because he was very scared, he pulled the trigger in self-defense and William Garrity was killed. There is nothing to show that Garrity was anything but a peaceable man. There had been no trouble between them. They had been the best of friends."

Redmond then claimed, "If Joseph killed Garrity it must have been in self-defense. For there was nothing in the evidence that showed any other motive. I ask that my client, Joseph Usher, be released on bail."

Judge Rall fixed the amount of Joseph Usher's bond at twenty-five thousand dollars. Redmond, now possessed most of the state's testimony; however, he had not disclosed the line of testimony for the defense.

Mekota was confident he presented a strong and effective case for the state since he had worked tirelessly and collected every scrap of evidence available. Since last Wednesday morning he had thrown himself into the case with diligence.

The preliminary hearing, he believed, had brought out the evidence fully and strongly.

Justice Rall ruled the case would be turned over to the Grand Jury in the fall because of all the evidence presented against Joseph Usher. Otto looked crestfallen. He was a stranger to the legal system, but he knew from the sound of things that his father was not coming home anytime soon. He watched as his father was led out of the courtroom and back to his dark cell for a brief stay. Now Joseph Usher would be transferred as a prisoner to the Marion, Iowa County jail until September.

After his father was taken away, Otto felt despair. He and his Uncle Isaac met with Defense Attorney Redmond immediately following the hearing, where they were told he would make an application to have the steep bond reduced. This gave Joseph's family a little hope and renewed their spirits as they went out into the driving rain to go back home. Uncle Isaac gave his nephew a pat on the back and tried to manage a weak smile.

Monday morning, no more than two days later, Attorney Redmond sent word to Otto that the dairy herd was sold. For Otto this was bitter sweet. He felt the burden of keeping up his father's dairy business—a herd of thirty cattle—while trying to focus on the legal proceedings and worry about Lucy and his little brother. Next week this would all change. Now there would be one less burden, but he knew his father would be devastated by the news of the sale. His father had deteriorated to the point where his son and brother didn't know if he had the strength to carry on. Otto knew Lucy's absence was probably best for her at this moment in time, and probably for Joseph, too, not having his young wife see him in this frail state.

# Chapter 20

By Sunday, June 14, 1903, two weeks had passed since the Lockwoods had taken Lucy to St. Luke's Hospital in Cedar Rapids for nervous prostration. Lucy was beginning to feel much calmer with all the care she had been receiving, along with the quiet and the rest. She could not remember a time when she had no chores to attend to—the washing, the cooking, the endless cleaning. For those two weeks, there was no one to look after but herself—at least physically. Of course, emotionally, she worried after Joseph and the boys, but behind the walls of the hospital, these familiar concerns seemed less dire.

The doctors had given her a complete physical, as well as taking her history along with her family's. Lucy cooperated in answering all their questions. She told her story of being raised in Appanoose County, Iowa by her parents, Albert Gillis and Eliza Ann Fleenor. Her father had been born in Pennsylvania, and her mother was a native of Iowa. Lucy told the doctors that she was the second born of ten children. One sibling had died at two weeks of age, from what was believed to be cholera, but the rest of her brothers and sister's were all mentally and physically healthy. This bode well for Lucy, since she came from strong stock.

Lucy had attended country school for several terms, and she considered herself to be bright, as well as lively and pleasant—although quiet in her nature. Lucy had always enjoyed society. In addition to her social nature, Lucy was naturally ambitious and industrious. She considered herself to be a hard worker, and she fared well in taking care of Joseph and the boys, as she had fared well in her previous roles where she was expected to be efficient and conscientious in her labors.

Lucy and Joseph had married when she was twenty-three years of age, and he was fifty, even though their marriage certificate stated her husband's age as only thirty-nine. She discussed her love for Joseph, despite the serious problems that they had encountered early on in their union. Lucy fretted over Joseph's affair with her younger sister, Hulda, and the resulting birth of an unwelcome child. She didn't know whom she felt betrayed by more—her husband or her younger sister of nearly six years. The sting and humiliation was doubly brutal.

Compounding this double betrayal was poor Otto, at the age of fifteen, being forced to marry Hulda. Lucy felt Otto was too young for this to have happened, but her father had insisted upon the unlikely union. No matter how hard Lucy tried, she returned to the dark feeling this affair had created, and she could find no way to fix the damage to her psyche or her family. But life continued, and in time Hulda and Otto's false marriage came undone; it was a marriage in name only from the start. And, over time, Joseph continually demonstrated his love and care for Lucy, and this helped to soften the ache of the affair.

After all, Joseph found his wife attractive; she was everything he desired in a woman—her black hair and brown eyes and slightly dark skin made her somewhat exotic and appealing. She stood no more than five foot two inches, and weighed a hundred ten pounds—which meant that Joseph could pick her up if need be, and this made him feel strong and manly in her presence.

Lucy's physical exam revealed she was pregnant since March, with an expected due date around the middle of November. This news shocked Lucy who realized she had not been feeling well for some time, but because of all the events and upheaval, she had not paid attention to herself. Suddenly, she longed to see Joseph and share her news. This should be a happy occasion, and yet, with Joseph being in jail, she was nervous about his response. Deep down Lucy believed it would all work out—she had to believe this or she would not be able to face the uncertain days ahead.

On Sunday, June 14, Albert Gillis was on his way to retrieve his daughter from the hospital in Cedar Rapids. He and Lucy's mother had been very worried about her mental state and how she would continue to fare throughout this tragic ordeal. They had decided they needed to bring Lucy back home until Joseph's release—if bail was made. When Albert entered Lucy's room, he was greatly relieved to find her serene, and sitting in the sunlight of the early day. She had color in her cheeks and smiled at the sight of her father.

Mr. Gillis agreed to bring his daughter to Marion, where Joseph was being held; the doctors explained to Lucy's father that they believed it would be helpful for her to see Joseph, since she missed him terribly and she had news to share.

Lucy took hold of her father's arm, and he led her outside. She squinted in the sun, and took in a deep breath of air, content to be outside of the hospital walls. Two week's time had passed quickly, and yet she felt it had been far too long since Joseph had wrapped her in his arms. By noon she and her father had arrived in Marion, where he made sure Lucy ate a good meal before they visited the County Jail. The doctors' instructions were for her to continue to get rest and eat properly. All Lucy desired was to lay her hands and eyes upon her husband, but she cooperated and finished every bite on her plate since her father watched her with concern.

At last they entered the County Jail, Lucy could not imagine Joseph passing his days locked inside. She only knew him as a man who spent his days outdoors, working with his hands, and coming inside for dinner smelling of livestock and hay. What could he be doing to pass away the hours? Her father worried for her and for her family. Lucy clenched her hands together, waiting for Joseph to be brought into the safe room. When he entered the room, they embraced one another and cried. Lucy was shocked at her husband's deteriorated state. She had thought of telling him her news, but now that she laid eyes upon his gaunt face, she thought better of disclosing her pregnancy. What really mattered now was that he saw she was feeling better and that his mind was set at ease by the color in her cheeks, and the clarity of her brown eyes. Lucy would wait until they were together outside these prison walls to tell him. Joseph let her know that his bothers, William and Isaac, felt they could have the bail money together very soon. This was hopeful news. They embraced, feeling the positive effects of even their short visit, which gave them each hope that they would be together in the not too distant future.

Even Mr. Gillis, gave Joseph his best, and shook his hand. He had forgiven past indiscretions and prayed that all would turn out all right for his daughter and her family. Lucy cried, as it was not easy for her to leave Joseph in the jail. He was so altered, all she longed to do was tend him and love him back to the man she had known before the murder of William Garrity. Mr. Gillis put his arm around his daughter's back and led her away from Joseph Usher. They had to say their goodbyes; a long journey lay ahead of them to their farm in southern Iowa.

# Chapter 21

On Monday, June 22, just a few days after Lucy's visit, Joseph was relieved to have his son, Otto, and Redmond visit him in the morning. Joseph was feeling frail; he knew his once sturdy body was breaking down since he had been placed under arrest.

Redmond left Otto with his father while he went on to see Judge Preston. This was the first time since the arrest that father and son were finally left alone to talk. There was comfort in this. Talking alone was something they had once shared each and every day, and now the simple act of privately conversing had become something unfamiliar.

The first thing Otto told his father was that the dairy business had been sold, and although this was somber news, one note of encouragement was that only one customer had stopped taking milk delivery due to William Garrity's murder. Otto reported, too, that the corn had been planted with the help of family, and the hired neighborhood men that Attorney Redmond had enlisted. Two cows had been kept for the family's needs, and the hog business was also kept since Otto was easily able to manage that end of things.

Joseph at last could confide in Otto. This was a great relief for the man. He explained to his son, who sat eagerly listening, what had transpired at the police station on the fateful day. He spoke softly about the morning of May 27, when he had finished delivering milk. He was actually on his way across the street to the police station since he wanted to speak to the officers; however, before he had made his way to them, they came to Joseph and escorted him to the station. He left the horses tied where Otto found them later that day. As soon as he entered the police station, the interrogation began and continued on and on. Joseph wisely decided he would make no statement to the authorities until he could consult his attorney and receive advice; however the police would not allow him an attorney at that time. They wore him out with questioning, and then began the threats and face slapping.

The Chief of Police came in and said, "Joe, now maybe you heard some strange noise upstairs. You went up there to see what the matter was. This man came at you. You saw this gun there and you grabbed it. You shot him in your own self-defense, in the defense of your wife and children.

"And if you wish to say that this is the way it happened, you may go to bed and get your rest. You can have your attorney in the morning."

At this point Joseph was so exhausted, he consented. He was fearful Lucy or even Otto may be blamed—especially Otto since it was his rifle that had been used. Joseph asked his son how he had fared through the whole questioning procedure, and Otto told him there was no fear as far as he was concerned. The police had asked few questions.

Otto and Joseph's private conversation ended here with Redmond's return. He needed to tell Joseph what had transpired. They had just filed a writ of *habeas corpus* in the district court, claiming the amount of bond was excessive.

County Attorney Mekota was present, and a showing was made on both sides. Judge Preston held that all defendants were entitled to bail except those charged with murder and treason. In murder cases the proof must be evident and the presumption great before bail could be denied. Judge Preston said the only evidence presented that Joseph had committed the killing of Garrity, was his own admission and it must be taken as an entirety. From the admission, the proof was not evident, nor the presumption great that Joseph had had a criminal intent.

Therefore the court had decided to reduce the amount of Joseph's bail bond from twenty five thousand to ten thousand dollars. Attorney Redmond informed his client that family and friends were signing his bond. Joseph would now be permitted to return to his farm, and in the fall he would be called to stand trial. When Joseph heard this news, he looked into his son's eyes, and for the first time Otto and his father felt a rush of hope pass between them.

Otto knew most of the men who had gotten together to sign his father's bail bond–Mr. Sam Smith, Mr. Del Wiltsie, Mr. Perry Usher, Mr. William Usher, and Mr. William Howard. Even though the mystery of Garrity's murder was unresolved, Otto felt support and sympathy from their neighbors and friends. Many were in agreement that not everything had yet been revealed. With the support of these men, the bail bond was approved and filed with the clerk of the district court.

Therefore, Sheriff Evans was ordered to release Joseph Usher, who was free to return home to his farm where he was to remain until his trial in September. The Sheriff told Redmond and Otto that Joseph had been a model prisoner who kept to himself, pacing the hall, and not speaking to the other prisoners. Now he would not have to pace any longer. Joseph left the jail with his attorney and his son by his side, and when he stepped out into the warm and open air, he took a deep, deep breath like a man who had nearly been drowned and just broken the water's surface. His voice trembled as he assured his attorney that he had remained hopeful all along; he had faith that his lawyers would succeed in reducing his bail bond so he could go home to his wife and sons.

Joseph was entirely grateful to the relatives and friends who had come to his rescue. He had his freedom for the summer, time to get his health back, and most importantly, time with his family at home to try and heal themselves in one another's arms.

# Chapter 22

When Lucy received the news that Joseph was released from the Marion County Jail, she had been home on her family's farm near Centerville, Iowa for a week. She and her father had driven into the farm yard with his favorite team of horses, and Lucy was touched as everyone ran out to greet her with the kind of hugs and smiles you can only find at home.

All of Lucy's exhaustion from her travels, and the emotional turmoil, was taken away by her family's welcome. There were tears in her eyes, but a newfound strength in her spirit. Just five minutes with her feet planted on the soil of her family's farm, and she knew how very much she had missed them all.

There was plenty to keep Lucy preoccupied that week. Her mother, Eliza Ann, needed help with the household, so her daughter, who understood the nature of work, did the daily chores alongside her. They washed the clothes by hand on the large washboard that her mother had used for as long as Lucy could remember. There was a comfort in the carrying out these familiar chores. The repetitiveness of the chores was like salve for Lucy's wounds, and even when her mother thought she should rest, Lucy insisted on working even more.

Her mother had noticed Lucy's clothes were filled out, and nothing she had brought with her was fitting properly. They spent the afternoons sewing up two new dresses and two new skirts for Lucy's now expanding figure. For Lucy, sitting side by side with her mother, and pulling the needle and thread through the cotton fabric, was a quiet meditation she was sorely needing. While they sewed tiny stitches, the bustling family life she had once been part of swirled on all around them—the voices, the stomping boots, the sounds of the chickens and cows outside—Lucy was joyful to be folded into the center of it all.

Two stormy days kept them in the house and the barns. This gave Lucy ample time to talk with her two brothers, George Albert, and Rymen, who had turned into young men in her absence and spent their days farming with their father, tending the livestock and working the fields. Lucy was proud to see how fine they were turning out. Martha Florence who was fifteen, helped her mother with all the household chores and sat sewing Lucy's new clothes and catching her sister up on all the local gossip. This was something Lucy had missed too. Their sisterly chatter flowed as if they had not spent a single day apart. After the storms had passed, Lucy was all to willing to head outside and play with her youngest siblings, Harry Lee, Pearl, and Daisy, who were still children with the energy Lucy had forgotten any little one could muster. Roscoe, who was on the cusp, just leaving boyhood behind, joined them in playing after his outside chores were done. Lucy could see he would follow after his older brothers; in character—he was already a hardworking member of their family.

As Lucy sat and sewed her new clothes, she envisioned the baby she would have with Joseph, and wondered if she would give birth to a boy or a girl. She longed for her baby to grow into a fine young boy or girl just as her siblings had, and she expressed these sentiments to her twenty-five year old sister, Sarah, who came with her husband Bill and their six children.

The visit was like its own little storm, with all of Lucy's nieces and nephews running about outside, climbing trees and chasing one another while screeching and hollering. Lucy's head was spinning just trying to keep their names straight—Ruth, Ruby, Kissie, William, George and John. Even her sister, Mary, came to visit, and Lucy got to hold her sweet baby daughter, Hazel, for the first time. Having all these children to focus on after two weeks in the hospital was refreshing, and when Lucy lay her head down on the pillow at night she was exhausted, but a healthy exhaustion, not the kind that had sent her to St. Luke's Hospital.

Lucy's mother raised baby chickens, and tended a large vegetable garden. All the children helped tending the garden, pulling weeds that never quit, and removing the rocks that cropped up out of the dark soil when no one was looking. Their meals were always delicious—especially Sunday, when her mother made her fried chicken, mashed potatoes, gravy and plenty of vegetables from their garden. For dessert there was homemade apple pie and sour cream cookies, and no matter where Lucy's travels had taken her, she had tasted none better.

The week had flown by, and all the loving distraction was good for Lucy. As she packed her bag, with her newly sewn dresses and skirts, she felt at peace. She had even had the opportunity to visit the grave sites of her brother, William, who had lived only six weeks, and her sister, Anna Lee, who had died eight years ago at only twenty-one years of age while giving birth to her daughter, Olive. Ann Lee's death had left a mark on Lucy. She missed her sorely, and leaving fresh lilacs on the graves of her siblings helped to bring her peace.

Hulda was the only sibling she had not seen, but when Lucy thought of her, she went straight back to that dark place in her mind. Really it was best she not let herself go there, and so she focused on other things, like her reunion with Joseph and the boys whom she had missed so very much. Lucy was eager to board the train, which would take her back to her husband so she could be in his arms and share her happy news. Her father called her to leave her childhood home. There were lots of hugs and tears as she said goodbye, and promises for visits soon to come. As Lucy's family watched her drive off with her father, they wished her well, and prayed all would work out for her family in the months to come.

# Chapter 23

Mid-September came far too swiftly. The days of summer had passed with the Ushers throwing themselves into their daily routines, and clinging to family and home with a new strength. Not until something is nearly taken from you, something you adore and take for granted is threatened to be gone, does the realization and appreciation truly come. The Ushers were given this opportunity, and with Joseph's return home, they clung to what they now knew to be all-important.

Joseph emerged from the tall, bustling corn stalks. The crop had grown well this season. He had been inspecting the ears, which were full and undisturbed by blight. The weeds were scarce in between the tall rows, and Joseph was proud of the hard work they had done on the farm since his release from jail. Working outside, breathing the open air, feeling the sun pulsing down on his strong back, had never felt quite this good. Every morning he awoke in bed next to Lucy, was a morning he was filled with gratitude, especially when he saw the swell of her stomach grow with their unborn baby.

As he stood just outside the field of corn, he sensed a change of weather. There was a brisk northern wind, picking up speed, and bending the stalks of corn in unison like golden waves. Chopping wood seemed in order, and this is how Joseph planned on spending the rest of his day. Fall was surely upon them.

Joseph was just about to call Otto to help him with the wood-cutting. They had some of their best moments chopping wood together. Something about the hard labor freed their tongues. And when they weren't talking, just being side-by-side, stacking piles of wood to keep them warm all winter, was enough. Joseph called his son's name and then glanced down the road, which was colored already with autumn's hues. He could see Redmond on horseback, making his way to the Usher's farm. A sick chill passed through Joseph. Without so much of an exchange his intuition told him what to expect. There are some visitors who bear bad news, and some doors that would be better off not being opened.

Redmond dismounted his horse and shook Joseph's hand. He asked his client if they could go inside to talk, since he wanted the Ushers to all be informed of the news at the same time. Lucy and Otto watched as Joseph and his attorney approached the farmhouse. There was a strong sense of nervous anticipation. Even with the calmness of summer, there was something unspoken that had loomed within the heart of each one of them. They knew unwanted change would be entering their lives once more.

Lucy collected herself and asked Redmond if he would like a hot cup of coffee; he gladly accepted since his hands were cold from his ride out to the farm. They all gathered around the table as the attorney explained the Grand Jury had been convened and they had reached their decision. A formal indictment had been returned against Joseph. He was charged with the deliberate, premeditated and willful murder of William Garrity.

With this news Lucy gripped Joseph's hands. Her heart fell as did her tears. Little Walter wrapped his arms around her. Otto stared down at the table-top, wishing for Redmond to leave, and with him, the bad news he had just dropped upon them. Joseph met his lawyer's gaze with strength. Lucy could not tell what was going through his mind since his eyes, nor his lips, nor his coloring betrayed a thing. He had become a master of keeping his emotions to himself. Lucy did not know if this was a blessing or a curse.

Redmond went on with his legal chatter. None of the Ushers could really take in his exact words. They each went in and out of comprehending. Lucy could see his lips moving but not discern the meaning behind his words. Joseph was advised not to give up hope. He would be defended with all the strength and energy his team of attorneys had. They were a team of prosecutors, recognized as the best criminal lawyers in the county.

The Ushers watched Redmond ride off down the road. As soon as he was out of sight, Joseph, Otto and little Walter headed to the woodpile. They used the two-man saw to cut the logs into pieces they could manage and then chopped those pieces with a sharp axe. This was a good outlet for all the frustration and upset they were feeling. Chopping wood was hard work and when they were done, they carried the stacks to the house and made a neat pile. This was a never-ending chore that none of them minded, especially today.

Lucy lay inside and listened to the rhythm of the wood chopping. Her hopes were devastated; she realized just how much she had blocked out the harsh realities facing them all summer long. Lucy had become good at this. She had done the same with Hulda, and now with Garrity's murder. As she lay alone, she realized she was not alone at all. Her little baby kicked strongly, almost as if keeping rhythm with the cutting of the wood. She placed her hands on her belly and closed her eyes on the afternoon light.

# Chapter 24

Autumn had settled over Iowa. On Friday, October 9, 1903 Redmond and the counsel for Joseph Usher prepared filed in the district court a motion for a continuance of the case, set for October 19, 1903.

The motion stated that Joseph's wife was in critical health, therefore his presence at home was necessary for the sake of his wife and unborn child. Other reasons for the request were the following.

*The charge made against Joseph Usher indicting him for murder of William Garrity in the first the degree.*

*That an indictment in said cause was returned against Usher at this term of court on the 15th day of September, 1903.*

*That many new additional points and facts are set forth in the minutes of the testimony attached to said Indictment, which will require investigation and time to prepare to properly meet and explain as way all of which this defendant can do.*

*But the time is too short now to meet the said facts and issues on the 19th day of October, 1903. This is the date upon which said cause is assigned for trial, having been assigned*

*by the court on notion of the county attorney without con-*
*sultation with the defendant or his counsel, and defendant's*
*knowledge until the 4th day of October, 1903, and without the*
*knowledge of his counsel until 3rd day of October, 1903.*

*That personally this defendant's health has not been good*
*for the past few weeks.*

*And that he has been suffering from some affliction of his*
*side and nervousness and he is not able at this time to give*
*proper assistance to his counsel in the preparation for or on*
*the trial of the cause. And he believes his ailment is temporary*
*and that he will be better able to make defense at the next*
*term of this court.*

*That defendant desires to make arrangements for assistant*
*counsel to aid in the defense of his cause, and for the first divi-*
*sion hereof, for the reasons assigned in this division, and for*
*the reasons to be assigned in the third division of this motion,*
*he is unable to make the necessary preparations for the de-*
*fense in the arrangement for counsel and preparation of de-*
*fensive testimony.*

*That it may be necessary (he is unable to tell at this time) to*
*obtain depositions of two or three witnesses who reside in the*
*city of Chicago, IL. And he is unable to state now whether their*
*attendance can be procured personally in his behalf, but is pro-*
*ceeding to determine that matter forthwith through his counsel.*

*That the defendant is wholly innocent of the charge made*
*against him in the above cause, and the time between the re-*
*turning of the indictment and that assigned for the trial is too*
*short to give him and his counsel opportunity to thoroughly*
*prepare his defense and to meet and explain the testimony*
*that may be introduced by the state.*

114

*That he is out on bail and will be, as he verily believes, ready for trial at the next term of the district court of the state of Iowa, in and for Linn county, of which county he has been a resident his entire lifetime.*

*Wherefore defendant asks in the interest of justice and that he may have a fair trial that said case be continued until the next November term of the Iowa district court within and for Linn County.*

# Chapter 25

By Tuesday, October 13, the Usher family had learned the disconcerting news that the motion for a continuance had been denied. If it is at all possible for a family to mourn the death of hope, this is how the Ushers felt. A quiet permeated their days; there was an understanding that no amount of talking would stave away the inevitable. Joseph's trial would begin in a mere few days, as soon as the Cistone case reached its conclusion.

With this understanding, Joseph made provisions for Lucy and the boys so that their suffering would be minimal in his absence. If he were found guilty, he would be under the direction of the court—no longer a free man, spending his days on the farm, carrying out the only labor he understood and adored. What concerned Joseph most when he considered his family faring without him were their warmth and their nourishment. Somehow he knew if these basic things were taken care of, he could find whatever slice of peace was possible in jail.

He made sure the men had the wood chopped into impressive piles, stacked neatly, and standing taller than him.

Joseph stood before the stacked wood and felt a sense of re-lief, knowing the fires would be kept burning throughout the unforgiving winter, when his infant would be taking those first breaths of life in Lucy's arms. Otto and Walter would not let their father down. They knew their chores well, and Otto had already proven how reliable he was last spring.

Joseph was proud of the young man his son was becom-ing, his sense of responsibility and strong work ethic. This week they were hand-picking the abundant corn crop from the fields, and Joseph was glad they were well under way. He knew, too, Lucy had the help of the neighborhood women who bustled about in the kitchen, standing over simmering pots on the stove, canning fresh fruits and vegetables from the garden. They had filled every glass jar, and then packed the cupboards until not another thing could fit. Joseph opened the cabinet doors and felt the same sense of relief as he did standing before the woodpile. He knew the neighbor-hood women would not let Lucy down.

They came often with bright chatter and sweet, handmade clothing for the baby. Joseph held the tiny outfits in his cal-loused hands and shook his head. No matter how many new-borns he witnessed come into this world, he never ceased to be amazed at how very wee they were. Lucy and Joseph were entirely grateful to their friends and neighbors. Joseph knew his wife was calmed by their kindness, and he made sure to show his appreciation in whatever ways he could think of—whether it be a generous word or a generous deed.

Word came that Joseph would be reporting to the district court around the 29th of October at which time he would be standing trial for the murder of William Garrity. The thought of this trial was almost incomprehensible to Joseph. He could make no sense of the process or what it would do to his family. There are things a man can learn to do without—like his dairy business, or even his dignity; however, Joseph could not comprehend making do without his family.

In support of their father, Joseph's daughter, Jennie, would be coming from Chicago to stay with relatives in Cedar Rapids. Jennie needed to be at her father's side throughout the trial. Joseph's oldest son, George, would also be coming from Chickasaw County. George would be a witness for the defense. The thought of Jennie and George being close by brought comfort to Joseph, Otto and Lucy.

There would be more love and support to get them through this ordeal. Joseph knew his life was in jeopardy, and he worried about this as well as Lucy's impending labor. He had no intentions of leaving his wife home without someone to be with her. All he knew for certain was that he could come home each day after court until the verdict was decided. God willing, the decision would be in his favor.

# Chapter 26

On Friday, October 30, 1903, Judge Thompson called his court to order at nine in the morning. Not until two in the afternoon was the selection of the jury completed. Once again, the courtroom was packed, as if the residents of Linn County had put their lives on hold to witness the Joseph Usher case. In some respects, this was, without doubt, the most sensational case in the county's history.

Judge Thompson called a half hour break after jury selection was final, and he instructed the court that County Attorney Mekota would give the opening statement on the state's behalf, followed by Mr. Redmond on behalf of Joseph Usher. The only sound you could hear when Mekota stood to address the jury, was the sound of breathing and the occasional cough or shuffling of feet on the wooden floor.

Mekota cleared his throat and adjusted the collar around his neck. Then he began his address to the jury. He read the formal indictment returned by the grand jury against Joseph. "They are charging him with the deliberate, premeditated and willful murder of William Garrity that happened on the night of May 26, 1903. In support of this indictment the state will produce evidence.

"William Garrity for a number of years was what we would call a 'farmhand.' He had no particular home. He had made his home with several of the farmers in that neighborhood. And he stayed with relatives either in Cedar Rapids or in Clinton Township. He would and did at times for several years work for Mr. Usher. He did farm work for some other friends in that locality. He was a man about forty years of age and was not married.

"Mr. Usher at the time this took place was a farmer and in connection with his farm ran a dairy. He sold and delivered milk in the city of Cedar Rapids.

"The evidence will show Mr. Garrity commenced to work for Usher this year in March.

"He worked there until the time that he was killed. He was killed on the night of the 26th of May, 1903.

"Between times he stayed out a few days. That Monday, May 25, one day before the tragedy took place out there, he went out with Mr. Usher, from Cedar Rapids. Usher coming in, saying that he wanted him to do some work on the farm. They came home on Monday night.

"The next day Usher went to town with his milk wagon, in the ordinary way. Mr. Garrity worked on the farm, cut wood and did some chores. Along about six o'clock Mr. Usher came home from his milk route. They did the chores, took their supper and retired about nine o'clock. It's as near as the evidence will show.

"There were at that time in the Usher family—Mr. Usher, Mrs. Usher, his wife, and two boys—Otto, aged about sixteen, and Walter, aged about nine. These four people, with Garrity, were the only persons in the house in the fore part of the night.

"The evidence will show they were the only people in the house when Garrity was shot. The evidence will further show that the little boy retired to bed first. That after him retired Mr. Garrity, who slept upstairs in a room. After Garrity went to bed Otto followed. Mrs. Usher and her husband went to bed last.

"This Usher home is in Clinton Township, about four and one-half miles west of Cedar Rapids. The house is an old-fashioned house. Garrity's room was upstairs. It was a very small room, about nine by ten feet, I believe. It had a little window on the south side and another on the west side. The approach to it was through stairs that were on the north side of the room. There is a railing around the stairs. As you go up into the room at the top of the stairs, there is a door leading into another room in which Otto and his brother slept."

Mekota then described the location of the beds in the rooms. "The beds are situated that their heads were together, with the partition between. The evidence will show that Otto, the oldest boy, was roused from his slumber by his father. His father said to him, 'Otto, get up, there is something wrong with Bill. Bill is dead.'

"Otto got up and they saw Garrity was bleeding profusely at the mouth and nose. I believe Garrity was nearly dead when Otto got up. They did some rubbing about his feet and head, and he expired soon after that. Then Otto went to the neighbors, to Spicer's. They live a quarter of a mile north of the Usher house.

"The hired man and Mr. Spicer came there between ten and eleven o'clock. Usher told them that Garrity had died of a hemorrhage. They believed him and did not go upstairs to see the body of Garrity. They did not go up until about three o'clock the next morning.

"When Mr. Gibney, another neighbor and, I believe, a distant relative of Garrity, came to Usher's house. He was telephoned for in some way.It was then the strangers, the people not belonging to the Usher family, went upstairs. They discovered Garrity lying on the bed, dead. He had his night clothing on, that is, his undershirt and drawers. The bedding covered with blood. Garrity was lying on his back, a little towards the front of the bed.

"Nothing took place and they said nothing. I think, until about twelve o'clock.

"Otto suggested that they send after the coroner in Cedar Rapids. The night was very stormy and the roads were frightful. It was one of the worst electric storms of the season. When they telephoned Coroner King he decided that the night was too bad for him to start out. He would go in the early morning.

"Word was also sent from out there to some relative of Mr. Garrity—a Mr. Warner—who employed Undertaker Ranck, was to go out there in the morning.

"Ranck and Warner got there about seven o'clock a.m. Their description of the body was about the same as given by Messrs, Gibney and Conley. They waited a little while.

"Ranck asked Usher whether it was murder, or natural death. He was assured that it was natural death. They waited for a little while. When coroner King did not come they concluded it was necessary to move the body. They put it in the wagon to go to Cedar Rapids. They were about a quarter of a mile from Usher's farm when they met Mr. King, the coroner, and told him what they had done.

"Mr. King drove on a little ways farther, and met Usher and Gibney. He had a conversation with them there. Usher assured him that Garrity had come to a natural death, that he had died of hemorrhage of the lungs, and Mr. King believed it.

"After a short conversation with them, he turned his horse around. He did not go to the Usher home but drove back to Cedar Rapids, following Mr. Ranck.

"After Mr. King and Gibney left, Usher went to the home of Mr. and Mrs. Spicer. He told the Spicer's and Ira Conley he desired them to go to his home to clean up the room in which Garrity died, and destroy everything there. He said there was lots of blood about the room. They would need pitchforks to handle the bedding.

"Mr. Conley, in carrying out this order, went to the Usher home between eight and nine o'clock a.m. Together with Otto he broke out the screen window in the west side of the room, took out the window, and through it he put the bedding, carpets, bedstead and spring. They burned the whole outfit in the road passing by the house.

"Ranck got to his undertaking establishment in Cedar Rapids with the body. They put it on the table and began to wash it off. Just about that time Coroner King arrived, and was anxious to see the body. It seems that there was some suspicion on the part of Mr. King as to why this strong able-bodied man had died so suddenly. Mr. Ranck, in taking the shirt from the body of Garrity, discovered a bullet wound. It was in Garrity's chest on the left side of the body. The wound was a little perhaps to the left of the nipple.

"Mr. Ranck said, 'Why, this man has been shot,' or words to that affect.

"As soon as Mr. King discovered this state of affairs, Mr. Ranck notified the authorities. He notified me.

"Mr. King went back to the Usher place. He also telephoned to Mr. Gibney. He seemed to take a good deal of interest in this matter. He was to meet him at the Spicer corner.

"Mr. King arrived there sometime during the midday, about twelve o'clock. He met Mr. Gibney and they went at once to the Usher home. When they got there all of those things taken from Garrity's room were already burned up. They could see the fire smoldering in the road.

"Mr. King then demanded of Mrs. Usher, or someone, to let him look into the room. When he went up there everything was gone. I think then Mr. King demanded to know whether there was a revolver on the place or any other firearms. They found a shotgun in Otto's room. The shotgun was hanging on the back of the bed in a case. He then discovered that Mr. Conley had taken part in the burning of these articles. He sent for him. Mr. Conley told the coroner that Otto had had a small rifle. He had seen it about five or six weeks before that.

"As soon as the coroner learned this fact, he wanted to know where the rifle was. He told Otto to go and get it. Otto went up to the room. When he came back he said. 'My God, my rifle is gone. I do not know where it is.'

"Then Otto, Coroner King, Conley, and Gibney began a search for the rifle.

"They found it in an oats bin slightly covered with oats. The oats bin is seventy-five or a hundred feet from the house. There was an empty cap in the rifle. Mr. King took possession of the rifle, and took the shell. He asked Otto if that was his gun. He said it was his gun.

"Mr. King and Mr. Gibney came back to Cedar Rapids. A warrant was issued for Usher that same day.

"Usher went to the city in the ordinary way that morning. He went over his route delivering milk as though nothing had happened. About four o'clock that afternoon he was arrested in front of the Arcade hotel. He was arrested by Marshal Kozlovsky. He was taken to the police station and asked if he had any statement to make. But Usher denied everything. He said he knew nothing about it. He still claimed that Garrity died of hemorrhage. He said he did not hear the shot and didn't know anything about it.

"After that interview the coroner and some of the other officials went to supper.

"Just before taking him back into the room the marshal took Usher into his private office. He asked him a few questions. In that conversation Mr. Usher admitted that he fired the shot that killed Garrity. That he did it with this rifle.

"I believe his explanation was that he heard some peculiar noise upstairs. He thought that one of the boys was sick. He went up to see if the boys were well. When he got into Garrity's room he saw the window on the west side was open.

"He repeated the same story after supper when the marshal called down the coroner. He also called the county attorney, newspaper reporters, and one or two other people. This was about eight o'clock in the evening.

"Usher made identically the same statement that he had made to Marshal Kozlovsky, only he went into more detail.

"This will be the line of evidence introduced by the state. We will endeavor to show that Usher did not kill this man in self-defense. That Garrity was murdered willfully and deliberately and while asleep in his bed. And that Usher is the man who did the shooting.

"There are certain things that cannot be explained.

"The state will be somewhat hampered. It will have to go into what we might call 'the enemy's camp' to get the evidence.

"There were only five people there, Garrity and the Ushers. The Ushers have been there ever since. The other man who was there is now dead.

"I think, gentlemen of the Jury, that we have evidence enough to satisfy you. A crime was committed, that it was willful and felonious, and that Mr. Usher did it."

With the indictment against Joseph, Mekota was finished with his statement.

Joseph sat stone still. Seemingly he was doing nothing more than blinking. Judge Thompson called for a dinner recess at this time, and the crowd began to stir as their attention broke and they thought of food and drink. Joseph's thoughts were elsewhere, although his family could not determine exactly where, just that he was far removed from the courtroom in which he sat.

# Chapter 27

The dinner recess lasted an hour and a half, after which time Judge Thompson called the court back to order. The crowd had returned after filling their stomachs while discussing the sordid details of the William Garrity trial. There was a quiet reverence in the room that far surpassed that of a church on Sunday morning.

Attorney Redmond now had a chance to begin his opening statement. He stood, took a deep breath, and turned to face the jury, who gave him their full attention. Joseph Usher's gaze also was riveted on his attorney. His hands rested on either leg, as if he were bracing for something—an earthquake or some other cataclysmic event.

"Gentlemen of the Jury, since three or four days after this unfortunate occurrence, I have been very closely associated with what has happened in this case.

I am gratified to know, now, that the county attorney—in making the statement to you in the closing confessed here— were many things that the state did not understand. But they thought they had enough to satisfy you that a murder had been committed. And that Mr. Usher was guilty of that murder.

"It is the first intimation from the state's side that has been fair to the defendant, Joseph Usher, whom they seek to charge and convict with murder. From the time he was taken into custody by the marshal of the city of Cedar Rapids, the conduct of the prosecution, in my opinion, has been more along the line of persecution.

"I am glad to know, in the closing sentences of the county attorney's remarks, he confessed. There is a weakness in the state's case. That weakness will be manifested as this case proceeds. We believe it will be manifested to such a degree as to lead you to believe that no crime has been committed.

"Let me call your attention now to this house the county attorney has described to you. He said it was an old-fashioned house. The house is L-shaped. The main part of the house is a story-and-a-half. It faces the road toward the east. The road in front of the house runs north and south. The house is on the west side of the road." Attorney Redmond explained in detail the arrangement of the room in the upper story of the Usher house, and supplied a sketch rendered by an artist of *The Gazette* staff one day following the shooting.

"Mr. Garrity was a man forty-four or five years of age. He had never been married. The evidence will show he was a man who consumed all his earnings in drink. That he worked from time to time about the country. That he was a goodhearted, quietly disposed man, harmless. Except that when he drank liquor, he became garrulous and contentious. He worked for Mr. Usher more or less for four or five years.

"There was never a word of trouble between them that anybody knows. It is a fact that there never was. Usher was kind to him, and he was kind and accommodating to Joseph Usher.

"In the last four or five years of his life, he had become practically be- bottled. He had been to some "cure" a time or two. But it did not seem to do him any good. A week or ten days before the night of this affair he asked for some money. He wanted to go to Cedar Rapids. Mr. Usher gave it to him. He went down town for the purpose of attending a circus. He stayed downtown, and he was intoxicated during the en- tire ten days as near as we can ascertain.

"As the evidence will show, on Monday evening, the 25th of May, he met Mr. Usher. Usher was driving home. Garrity said that he was ready to go home. Usher said he was glad of it. He being a milkman, he was obliged to deliver milk. He did not get home until late at night.

"That night Usher told Garrity he would be glad to have him go home with him. They went home together. Garrity came to where Usher was sitting on the front porch. He wanted to know if he, Usher, had heard them say anything about him, Garrity, near around the Arcade hotel. He want- ed to know if they had told him any stories about him. Mr. Usher told him that he had been too busy delivering milk. He didn't have time to stop and listen to any stories. Garrity said but little. He complained some that he was not feeling well.

"The next morning Mr. Usher was obliged to leave the farm in order to deliver milk to his customers. He left in- structions, if Garrity was able to do anything, he might do the chores, possibly cut some wood or poles. Mr. Usher did not know what Garrity did on the farm that day. Mr. Usher was a man who attended strictly to his own business and worked hard. Nobody knew the route but Mr. Usher. Other people could not go over it, without having had a day or two experience on the wagon.

"The boy, Otto, a young man of sixteen or seventeen years, that day loaded a load of hogs. Otto took them to town. It is to be presumed that Garrity probably helped him load the hogs. During the afternoon Mr. Garrity acted queer. In the evening, when Mr. Usher got home, along about seven o'clock, they had supper. Garrity ate but little, and wasn't feeling very well after eating supper while Mr. Usher was out cleaning the milk cans at the well. He was taking care of his milk as he usually did.

"He spoke to Garrity once or twice but received no response. Garrity finally looked up in his face and said, 'Joe, do you see anything in the air here?'

"Mr. Usher said 'No'

"'Yes, you can see it over there by that tree–don't you see it over there?'

"'Where is it?' inquired Mr. Usher.

"'Right there by that tree,' replied Garrity.

"Usher looked at him. He thought Garrity must see something that he (Usher) could not see. As he walked over to the tree he said, 'I don't see anything except that knot.' Or something of that kind, which he pulled off and threw down. 'Why,' he said to Garrity, 'there is nothing here, you must be sick.' Then Usher said, 'You go to bed, there is certainly something wrong with you.'

"Garrity left Usher there.

"Usher took a lantern when he went to the barn to do the chores. He usually did.

"Garrity went into the house. While he was there he went up to Otto who was reading by the kitchen table. He said to him, 'Otto, do you think they could do anything with a fellow that had said something. About somebody, could they hang him or put him in the penitentiary?'

"Otto said, 'No Bill.'

"Then Garrity said, 'Can I have your shotgun? I will go into the cellar and they cannot get me there. I can fix them if they do.' Or the words were to that effect.

"Usher, soon after that, came into the kitchen with the lantern. Garrity asked him if he might take the lantern. It was very unusual for him to take a light. He only did this once in a while to change his clothes by. He also took a two-quart cup full of water.

"Shortly after Garrity retired Otto went to his room. He went up the stairway and through Garrity's room. He noticed that Garrity was on the bed in his nightclothes. He had on his day shirt and his drawers. He made some remark about the mice being thick. Bill said something, but Otto doesn't remember what it was. The lantern was burning on that chest. It was just as Garrity had left it when he went to bed. Right immediately west of the chest was a lot of old clothes.

"Otto went to bed. Mr. Usher went to bed downstairs. They slept near the kitchen in the 'L.' Their little boy had been suffering from the croup. Some times in the night Mr. Usher would hear noises in that room upstairs. He had a short time before this occurrence gone up there to take care of the little boy. He went to see what the matter was with him.

"Later as Joseph was dozing he heard a noise and located it in that room. It was a scraping, groaning noise. He left his wife and started up the stairway. He was intending to take care of the little boy. When he got to the head of the stairs he saw the lantern. And saw that Garrity was on the bed. He looked to the right. Knowing the window was open and it was storming he concluded to step over there. And he put it down. While he was over there putting down that window, and before he had gone into his son's room, and while he had his hands on the window, in the act of putting it down, he heard a noise behind him which he supposed to be Garrity moving in the bed. Or possibly Garrity was getting out of it. He did not pay much attention to that. He kept on putting down the window.

"When he turned around Garrity was getting out of bed, or he had his feet on the floor.

"Garrity was, unfortunately, the victim of alcoholic insanity. He had persisted in his carousals until his mind was practically gone. And his health was affected.

"It is well known that people like him suffer from various hallucinations. Sometimes they believe that persons are organizing against them. Sometimes it takes the form of wanting to kill everyone. More often it takes the form of the hallucination. They believe that it is necessary to protect themselves.

"This was the form of Garrity's alcoholic insanity. He imagined that someone was trying to do him harm. He thought someone around the Arcade hotel was after him.

He asked Usher that night on the porch if he heard them talking about him the Arcade hotel. He had asked Otto If he thought they could do anything for something he said.

"The evidence will satisfy you, without any doubt, that this was his condition. Garrity, in his beset condition, imagined that someone was after him. Garrity, poor fellow in his delusion rose from his bed.

"Now Garrity was familiar with a small rifle.

"It had been in the possession of Otto Usher about sixty days. It was a light, target rifle, 22 caliber shot. Garrity and the boy, Otto, had used it in shooting at ground squirrels. They also used it shooting at a mark.

"Garrity knew where the gun was hung in the front room over Otto's bed. Garrity was familiar with that rifle. He knew where the ammunition was. He was never seen to handle a gun or any weapon of that kind.

"Now, as Usher closed the window and squared himself around, he saw Garrity getting out of bed. He noticed Garrity in this condition, (partly stooping). This position of Garrity attracted Usher's attention to something bright lying on the bed. Garrity was reaching for it.

"Then Usher noticed that it was a gun. Now, the evidence will show that Usher is a very nervous man, extremely, excessively nervous. He then became frightened. There was some oath from Garrity, which Mr. Usher cannot remember, and then he said, 'Now, I've got you and I am going to kill you.'

"That frightened Mr. Usher until he lost all control of himself. He read in Garrity's insane condition, in his glaring eyes, what he had said at the well–that this man was practically a maniac.

"There was a race for that gun between Usher and Garrity.

"Usher got it first and in the tussle it was discharged and Garrity fell back on the bed.

"Usher was not sure the other man had been shot or that he was dead. He got up in a dazed sort of a way.

"He was not sure that Garrity had been shot until the next afternoon. As he himself said he was a weak, nervous shadow. He thought to himself, now this man, this maniac may come at me. He could kill me and kill my whole family. He thought the gun was loaded with more shells. In his state of mind then he didn't know but it had forty shells.

"The thought that ran through Usher's mind was that Garrity was coming at him with that gun and so it was that Usher fled downstairs, without his clothes.

"He went through the kitchen, out into the darkness and the storm with that rifle.

"Threw it into the oats bin and closed the door upon it. The statement that it was covered with oats is not true. The oats had been taken out of the bin. There were a few left, those between the cleats on the bottom of the bin. Usher threw the gun into the corner and then ran back to the house. He was completely overcome.

"He isn't clear about what he did for the next twelve or fifteen hours. He went into the house in a dazed sort of a way and roused his family. He didn't know what to do. He aroused Otto and told him that Bill was dying. There was no evidence then that he had shot Garrity. And anyway he wasn't thinking about that at the time.

"He asked Otto to bathe Bill's face and Usher rubbed Garrity's feet, crying. He called, "Bill" several times but it soon became apparent that Bill was dead.

"Mr. Gibney was notified and the coroner sent for at the request of Usher himself. No one knew what had happened exactly. There was confusion and excitement, more or less, that night.

"But in the morning the coroner didn't get there and the undertaker was on hand.

"Mr. Ranck went up there and took the body without waiting for the coroner to come.

"They took the body against the protests of Usher. No fewer than three times Usher told him to wait for the coroner.

"Usher was under the impression that there should be an inquest. He thought that he should not say anything about the facts until the inquest was held. That was why he went through the storm to telephone for the coroner.

"He said to Ranck, 'Can't we have an inquest here?'

"But Mr. Ranck replied, 'It could just as well be held over town.' Then they went away with the body.

"Usher went on his milk route. It was his expectation to go to the coroner and tell him what had happened. He never used the word hemorrhage in speaking of Garrity's death. He said that Garrity had bled to death, which was literally the truth. He didn't know that he had shot Garrity then. He was about to go to the coroner's to inquire about the inquest.

"He proceeded along the line of his supposed duty, when he was just about to go and tell the coroner. After he had finished his milk route that day, he was arrested by Marshal Kozlovsky and was taken to the police station. The marshal told him that they did not mean him any harm. If he had anything to say, he ought to tell them the truth.

"Mr. Usher said, 'Now I am under arrest. I don't know that I ought to talk to you without an attorney. But if it is your judgment, then I will tell the truth.'

The marshal then telephoned for the coroner, the county attorney, and two newspapermen to be present. When they arrived the marshal brought in Usher.

"He said, 'Here is the coroner. We would like to have you tell him what you told me.'

"Mr. Usher said, 'Can't I have an attorney?'

"And the marshal said, 'Yes, guess you can have an attorney if you want one. We would like to have you tell the coroner the truth as you told me.' Then Coroner King administered the oath. Usher raised his hands to high heaven. What he said was taken down in shorthand by Mr. Holmes here. And it was extended into long hand. It will be offered in evidence to this jury.

"Usher thought that was the time to tell the truth before Almighty God, and respond to the questions of the county attorney, the coroner and the marshal. That is the whole truth. Contrary to the usual order of things, we want that confession here in evidence. We want every word of it.

"Mr. Usher held to that statement. For that statement is true and there is no other evidence. Usher isn't guilty. He told the truth just as it was. It is true– every feature of it.

"The County Attorney has stated to you something about burning clothes. That is true, too.

"In his nervous excitement he met the coroner. He didn't go back to destroy the evidence. He went to Mr. Spicer's, his neighbor. He said he would like the hired man, Mr. Conley, to help Otto clean the room. There was an old blood- soaked straw tick and some blood- stained bedding. He didn't tell them to burn the bedstead or the carpet. They cleaned up the room according to their own idea of it. He did tell them to use a pitchfork. He didn't want them to handle that clothing. The reason for this will be made apparent, when we use details of the testimony.

"Usher was ignorant for the way Conley and Otto cleaned up the room. He gave some general directions how it should be done. He wanted the room cleaned like it had been after the death of his first wife. She died two or three years before.

"It is not true that Garrity's clothes were burned. They all hang there now just as they did then, except what he wore when the body was taken to the undertaker.

"Usher has suffered much from this. He was guilty of no intentional crime. There never was a conviction in this kind of a case without a motive being shown. No man ever killed another man without a motive.

"The state said that there was something strange about this case. There is something strange about it. We think that when the evidence is all in, it will be clear that Usher is a most persecuted wrecked man over this. That he had no control over and no purpose to commit."

Redmond ended his statement with this last effective point and sat down. Joseph felt relief that the long session of the past two days had reached its conclusion, although his intellect told him that he may be going from the frying pan straight into the fire. His family, too, was glad for the respite from the courtroom, providing them a chance to catch their collective breath. There was an odd sensation shared by the Ushers that they were out to sea, all of them together, flailing about in the inhospitable and dark water. A deep dread seeped into their hearts, along with the chill air that warned of winter's descent.

The Ushers arrived to a warmed house, with Lucy happy to greet her family and the smells of her cooking wafting out through the front door. They stomped the dirt off the bottom of their boots and sat down to a hot meal. Lucy's kitchen chores were difficult to carry out now that she was towards the end of her pregnancy. Her baby kicked much of the time, or shifted around in what little space was left, and this movement made resting a challenge. Little Walter was good to help her out and his willingness to lend a hand made his father proud.

At a time of such misfortune, the Ushers found plenty to be grateful for, and the hard work provided by Joseph's brothers—Isaac, William, along with their sons, made it possible to keep things running on the farm. All those hands completed the picking of the field corn, and ensured it was stored in the corncrib for the winter, out of the harsh elements. By Wednesday, the Ushers looked around the property and knew everything was done and preparations were made for winter. There were things that could not be controlled, like the murder case of William Garrity, but the things that could be taken care of were, and that would have to suffice for the time being.

# Chapter 28

When Wednesday, November 4, arrived, the district courtroom was filled to capacity when the proceedings resumed by nine in the morning. The Ushers had hoped the curiosity would have died down by now, and that the community would have gotten back to their routines, and busied themselves with the approaching holidays. This was not the case. Joseph realized human nature dictated love for the sensational—that he was at the center of the storm was most unfortunate for himself and his family. Joseph made a quick sweep of the courtroom spectators and saw both Reverends, Lockwood and Mershon, pastors from the Methodist Churches in Cedar Rapids. Even men of the clergy were not above a thirst for the local murder case.

Judge Thompson noted the jurors were seated and inquired of counsel if they were ready to proceed with the examination of witnesses. Joseph's family could see him withdraw, like a hunted animal into its hole. His glaze fixed downwards and his posture deflated as if the weight of Cedar Rapids rested on his tired shoulders. Mekota asked a number of witnesses for the state to be sworn, and then he called Ira J. Conley to the stand. At this point, much to Joseph's dismay, the real trial was commenced.

Mekota began questioning Conley, who was showing his nerves with a red face and edgy demeanor. He sat on the edge of his seat and testified:

"I live at George Spicer's. The farm is six miles west of Cedar Rapids. I have worked there eighteen months, and have resided in Linn County all my life. Spicer's farm is a quarter mile north of Usher's on the same road. I was working for Spicer's on May 26, 1903."

He swallowed hard and then went on to repeat his story of arriving at Usher's the night of the murder, and going up to see the body.

Mekota inquired, "How did you find Garrity and describe what you saw."

Conley responded, "Garrity's body lay on his back, partly covered. He had on underclothes and outside shirt. His right hand was down by his side, his left hand was across his breast, to the right of the middle. His face was turned straight up. His head was towards the head of the bed. He was lying towards the front rail of the bed. I did not have a conversation there with Usher about Garrity's death. It was not referred to after that. When Gibney came, Usher said that Garrity's death must have resulted from hemorrhage, caused by hard drinking. I last saw Garrity alive on May 19. It was about five o'clock a.m. when I went home. I left Mr. Weed and Gibney with the Usher family. Usher came to Spicer's between eight and nine that morning. He wanted me and Mrs. Spicer to go up and clean the room. He asked us to use a pitchfork in handling the bedding. And to burn it, which we did. The bedding was blood-stained. There was a small chest, a telescope grip and some old clothes in the room. We didn't touch the clothing. After burning the bedding, carpets, etc., I went home.

"I returned to the Usher's about noon on request of Coroner King. Otto, Walter, Mrs. Usher, Mr. Gibney and the coroner were there."

Conley straightened in his wooden chair and described the search for Joseph's gun, which he realized when he found —it, belonged to Otto.

At this time, Mekota had no further questions for Ira Conley. The jurors had been listening intently through the testimony. When Major Smith began the cross-examination, the jurors seemed to become even more astute, sitting taller and focusing in on the witness at hand.

"I have known Garrity eight or nine years. But had never been friends with him. I am twenty-nine years of age. I figure Garrity was about forty."

Conley reiterated his testimony regarding Usher's statements concerning the cause of Garrity's death. He said: "I did not ask to go up to see the body. I am perfectly familiar with the house, having worked there for a time. I have occupied the room Garrity was killed in. Usher went to Spicer's about eleven o'clock in the evening. On returning Usher said he had telephoned the coroner and Mr. Gibney. Mr. Weed, the second person to arrive, was summoned by Otto. The nearest telephone was at Spicer's. It was about three a.m. when Gibney came. Usher went down to Spicer's again. He went to see if they had sent word to the coroner and to Mr. Gibney. On his return he said he was tired.

"Garrity's room was about seven feet wide and nine feet long. When I went up with Gibney and Usher they took a lantern with them. The room was dark except for the light of the lantern."

At this time Conley was shown a plan of the rooms like the one shown in *The Gazette* the previous Saturday. He looked over the sketch and said, "This is correct. There was a chest in the room. It sat two and a half or three feet from the bed, the head of which was against the partition. The foot was about two and a half feet from the window, the sill of which was eighteen to twenty-four inches from the floor."

He then repeated his statement about the position of Garrity's body at three o'clock. He was the first person outside of the Usher family to view the body, and he let it be known that no words were exchanged while they were upstairs in Garrity's room.

"Usher told us about the efforts they made to restore Garrity. I can't say just when he made that statement. He said they bathed his head and rubbed his feet. They called to him, but received no answer. The only bedding over Garrity's body was the corner of a quilt. It was over one knee. The bedding was rumpled and thrown toward the back of the bed. Usher told me that Walter had been carried downstairs, asleep. I was not surprised that Usher wanted the room cleaned the next morning."

Major Smith then asked him, "Did you not know that Garrity was suffering from a loathsome disease?"

However, the objection of counsel for the state was sustained.

142

Conley continued, "When Usher asked us to go up and clear the room, he said he did not want Otto to get any of the blood on him. Usher told us that we should use a pitchfork. But he made no explanation for that peculiar request. Mrs. Spicer went up with me to help clean up the room. Mr. Ranck had been there and taken the body away.

Otto helped take out the bedding, bedstead, and carpet. We took them into the road and burned them. Mrs. Usher told us to burn everything, carpets and all. The third visit I made to Usher's was in company with Mr. Gibney and Coroner King. I knew Otto had a target rifle, for I have seen it, loaded it and shot it."

Major Smith then asked for the gun, which the state produced after some objection, and the weapon was identified by Ira Conley. The witness testified: "The gun was in a dark corner of the granary when I found it. There were but a few oats in the bin, and it was down into them. I handed the gun to the coroner. Usher went to town on his milk wagon via Spicer's. It was about eight o'clock that morning, and I did not see him again that day. I have never seen anything in the way of trouble between Usher and Garrity. There was some talk that night about Garrity being a hard drinker. I knew Garrity drank, but only when he went to town."

With no further questions Ira Conley was dismissed. He made his way off the stand and was relieved to be done, relieved not to have a courtroom full of people focused on him and waiting on his every measured word.

He and Otto had been good friends. He did not want any harm to come to the Ushers due to his testimony. He cared for the Ushers and had respect for Joseph. During his time on the stand, he knew he had told the truth to the best of his ability; he only hoped his words would not effect Joseph in any negative way.

The next witness called was Eabert Weed; Mekota began the questioning. Weed testified, "I live in Clinton Township and I am a farmer. I have resided where I now live for fifty years. My house is one hundred-twenty rods from Usher's. I was there on the night of May 26, 1903. Otto came up and asked me to go. I was in bed, but got up, dressed and went to Usher's farm at twelve o'clock. It was raining hard and the ground was covered with water. Usher, Conley and Mrs. Usher were there when I arrived. Usher was talking in the sitting room with Conley.

"I spoke of the sudden death of Garrity. Otto had told me Garrity had died of hemorrhage. Usher said he must have died suddenly. No one asked me to go upstairs. Usher suggested that I lay down in the room with Walter, which I did. He talked about what could cause hemorrhage of the lungs in a man like Garrity. Mr. Gibney came while I was lying down. Usher appeared somewhat nervous."

On cross-examination by Major Smith, Weed said, "Usher has lived neighbor to me for a number of years and I have known him all that time. He is naturally a nervous man. I got up about five o'clock, saw Gibney there. Garrity has worked for me at times. He was a man who drank occasionally. Garrity would go to Cedar Rapids on a 'spree' once in a while. I asked whether they would not need the coroner. Mrs. Usher said they would, that 'it was law.' She said Mr. Gibney had been requested to notify the coroner.

Later Usher asked Otto to go to Spicer's, and see if word had been sent to the coroner, but instead went himself."

After this brief testimony Eabert Weed was dismissed and Mekota called Mr. Gibney to the stand. The witness was asked where he lived and how he knew William Garrity.

Mr. Gibney testified as follows: "I live a mile and three quarters north of the Usher farm. I am a farmer. I have known Usher for twenty or twenty-five years. I have known Garrity for as long as I can remember. His mother is a first cousin of mine."

Mr. Mekota asked. "When did you learn about Garrity's death?

"I was called by telephone by George Spicer and I learned that Garrity was dead."

"What did you do after you had received the call?"

"I went to Covington to notify Garrity's sister in Cedar Rapids, and notified the coroner. I returned home and went to Usher's. I received three messages from Spicer's that night. I talked with Ira Conley first, then with Spicer, later with Usher.

"Usher asked me if I would come to his place before daylight. He said Garrity was dead and asked if we hadn't better call in the trustees. I told him that I had notified the coroner, and that Garrity's mother would probably bury the body."

"When did you go to Usher's?"

"About three o'clock a.m. May 27. Usher, Otto and Ira Conley were there. I didn't see Mrs. Usher. They were sitting in the front room. I asked Usher if he had room in the barn for my horse. He sent Otto to put the horse up.

"Usher said he heard a noise upstairs and thought it was Walter. He went up and found Garrity about dead from hemorrhage. And that they bathed his head and rubbed his feet."

"When did you see the body and how did you find it?"

"I suggested that we go up and see the body. Usher and Conley went up with me."

Mr. Gibney then detailed the position of the body on the bed. His testimony was exactly like that of Mr. Conley. He said he could remember of no conversation in the room. Mr. Gibney stated, "When we went downstairs I told Usher he better go upstairs and that he should open a window in Garrity's room. A little later Usher went to lie down. I talked with Mr. Conley and went down to Spicer's about six o'clock. I returned to Usher's and stayed until the body was taken away by the undertaker.

"Mr. Ranck, arrived about six o'clock. Louis Werner came with Ranck. Ranck asked Usher if this was murder or a natural death. Usher said it was natural death. He supposed it was a hemorrhage, as Garrity drank hard. Ranck was there about half an hour. Mr. Ranck suggested that the body be taken away. Usher made no objection, but said he would like to have Mr. Weed there. He wanted everybody satisfied that everything was all right. Mr. Gibney and Werner helped carry the body down. Usher went part way upstairs and then turned back. Mr. Ranck told them not to move or touch anything in that room. Not until the coroner came, he would be there soon. Usher and I left the place together.

"Soon after Ranck left, Usher was walking and I was on horseback. We met Coroner King on the road and talked with him fifteen or twenty minutes. The coroner asked Usher as to the cause of Garrity's death. He made a statement about how they had found him upstairs. Usher said that he was a hard drinker. Usher said he supposed Garrity's death was brought on by hard drink. That he had not been feeling well for some time. I then went home. Mr. King went to Cedar Rapids and Usher was standing on the corner. My impression is that Usher said that Garrity died of hemorrhage.

Mr. King said he would have to follow the body into Cedar Rapids, and give a burial permit.

"I returned to Usher's about eleven o'clock to meet Mr. King. He had phoned me to go back to the Usher's farm to look for a gun—a rifle. Mrs. Usher and Otto were there. Mr. King and I went into the room. We found nothing there but items of Garrity's clothes. We spent some minutes in looking for the gun. Otto said he didn't know where it was. Conley found it in the oats bin. Otto said it was his gun. He had been looking for it for a half hour."

The judge adjourned for lunch at noon, and he warned the jury not to discuss the case. Joseph was taken from the courtroom to have his meal and get some rest. His family gave him sympathetic glances as they stood and waited for Joseph's exit. They noticed how nervous-looking and pale he was. The break would be short, just an hour, before the cross-examination was scheduled to begin by Major Smith. None of the Ushers had much of an appetite but they all were happy to leave the confines of the courtroom where the air and the tension got way too close.

Thomas Gibney stated on cross-examination, "Garrity was a single man, about forty-three years of age. He was about five feet ten inches in height. He would weigh about one hundred fifty pounds. He had made his home at Usher's 'off and on' for several years. When I received the first telephone message I understood the message came from Usher. It was to the effect that Garrity was dead and he wanted me to come to his place. I tried to get Covington by phone, and then went there afoot. I wanted to communicate with Garrity's sister.

While at Covington I talked with Spicer by phone. Spicer said Usher thought they ought to have the coroner and myself. Then we should call up Dr. King. I returned home and then talked directly with Usher. Usher asked me to come over before daylight. Also he asked whether they hadn't better call the trustees. In that conversation Usher said nothing about the coroner."

Gibney then detailed the conversation between Undertaker Ranck and the defendant, adding nothing to what he had said on direct examination. When asked whether Usher objected to having the body removed, Gibney answered, "No, sir, I can't say that he did."

Gibney was asked, "Didn't Usher ask if the inquest should be held at Usher's farm home?"

He said, "No, Mr. Usher didn't."

On re-direct examination Gibney said, "I had seen Garrity the Saturday previous to the day of the death (Tuesday)."

Questions as to Garrity's condition on that day were objected to by the defense and then sustained by the court.

Gibney stated, "When Usher laid down that night he asked to be called at four o'clock, I suggested that we go upstairs to see Garrity's body."

On re-cross-examination Mr. Gibney denied Usher ever asked him if he wanted to see Garrity's body. Mr. Thomas Gibney was then released from the stand.

At two o'clock when the next witness, George Spicer, was called to the stand, Mekota began the questioning.

He testified as to the location of his farm with reference to the Usher place. He detailed how Otto Usher came to his home between nine and ten o'clock.

Mr. Spicer stated, "The defendant came down half an hour later to borrow some kerosene. Usher told me about Garrity's death."

His statement differed in no material respect from what had already been detailed by the other witnesses.

Mr. Spicer continued: "Usher came back about twelve o'clock and wanted to talk with Mr. Gibney. I called Gibney up. Usher went home and returned between two and three o'clock. He came in from the rear through the kitchen and into my bedroom. He was excited and nervous. I again asked how Garrity came to his death. I said. 'I suppose it was sort of a hemorrhage.' He said, 'I guess it was.' I then suggested that Garrity might not be dead. Usher said he knew he was.

"I suggested a possible suicide, but Usher said it was not suicide. He came back about eight o'clock in the morning. He asked Conley and my wife, Mrs. Spicer, to come up to his house. He said the family needed help to clean up the room."

On cross-examination Mr. Spicer stated, "When I talked with Mr. Gibney over the phone, I told that gentleman that Usher wanted to summon the coroner and undertaker."

With no more questions, Mr. George Spicer was excused from the stand.

Joseph watched his neighbor as he passed and thought how odd it was to be side by side in a courtroom instead of standing out in the country, mulling over livestock or crop matters. Joseph's life had become unrecognizable and the relationships he had known were no longer familiar. The night Garrity died, all Joseph had known and counted on was altered. Bill died, but in a sense, Joseph felt his life was taken too.

True, he was still breathing, still able to eat and sleep and dream, but all was disrupted, contaminated, and Joseph longed for his previous life to return. If he could turn back time, he would have kept William Garrity at arm's length, and never had the man sleep beneath his family's roof.

Joseph glanced around the courtroom, after George Spicer took his seat, and he took in the crowd, all the available standing room was occupied, and many were women. He fixed his gaze downwards once more; it was far easier to stare at the floor or the tabletop than it was into the curious and prying faces of his neighbors.

# Chapter 29

This particular day in court dragged on longer than the others for Joseph. The testimony was drawn out and was accounts Joseph had already heard. He felt like the attorneys were beating a dead horse, but there was nothing he could do to speed along the legal process or make any kind of sense out of it. There was such clarity now for Joseph Usher and why he had preferred the simple life of being a farmer, preferred working for himself, and having only himself to answer to; there was no bureaucracy in working a farm, just honest sweat and hard labor. These were the things Joseph understood.

Mekota called Undertaker Courtney Ranck to the stand, and as predicted by Joseph, his testimony was the same as he had given at the inquest. He talked about being called to Usher's house, about the funeral being held in Kenwood, arriving, seeing the body and deciding to take it to the city.

He described the position of the body, and how he had discovered the bullet hole in Garrity's chest.

"Coroner King was angry with me and asked if I regarded it as complying with the law. He said I should not have removed the body before the arrival of the coroner. In view of all the circumstances and the wish of the dead man's relatives, I thought my actions were perfectly proper. I told the Ushers not to remove any of the clothing or bedding until the arrival of the coroner."

Cross-examination was brief. Ranck stated, "In taking off the shirt I did not see any powder burns."

Following this statement, Mr. Ranck was excused and stepped down.

Coroner David W. King was the next witness called to the stand.

County Attorney Mekota began by asking Mr. King to "Describe the events of the morning of May 27, 1903."

King repeated his previous testimony about being called to the Ushers' and discovering the body had already been taken away.

"I then returned with the undertaker to make a through examination of the body. It did not take long to discover that Garrity had been shot through the left breast. I returned at once to the Usher home. I was in disbelief. I found that in the brief time since the removal of the body every vestige of furniture in Garrity's room had been burned. Even the clothing of the deceased had been added to the fire. The floor and woodwork of the room had also been cleaned.

"I interrogated Mrs. Usher, Otto and nine-year-old Walter. I told them that William Garrity had been murdered. They all denied any knowledge of the tragedy. Mrs. Usher told me that she didn't know anything about a gun. She said she had not heard a gun discharged the night Garrity met his death and she declared that Garrity had not been killed. About this time Ira Conley, the young man employed by Mr. Spicer, a neighbor of the Usher's, told me Otto Usher had recently bought a target rifle. I asked Otto where it was and told him to go get it."

He described the search for the rifle and how Conley had found it. "I then asked Mrs. Usher and Otto a few more questions. I told the family 'I am afraid that a murder has been committed.'

"I got onto my cart and drove back to town. When I returned to the city, I found that Dr. King had completed the postmortem examination of the body. He had found the bullet, a 22-short. It was just beneath the skin in the middle of the back. The bullet had entered the left breast, passed through the left lung. It glanced down the spinal column and stopped at a point opposite the eighth dorsal vertebrae. Dr. King told me that death had resulted from hemorrhage, caused by the wound. I at once filed on this information before Justice Rail."

Mekota then dismissed his witness, as there were no further questions. Joseph looked for his son. He had a sense of what was to follow; Otto was to be questioned, and his father felt the need to give him a reassuring smile before he took the stand. Joseph located his son in the midst of the crowd, even though his eyesight was blurred from fatigue and focusing downwards for so long a stretch, but he could still determine that Otto was exhausted from sitting long and listening hard to the proceedings all day. Earlier that morning Otto had been sworn in. Joseph thought what a strange idea to have his son take an oath to speak the truth—the truth perhaps being the very thing that would help put his father behind bars.

Attorney Crosby began questioning Otto. Joseph was proud of his son. He saw a softening in the crowd as they took in Otto's youth and handsome demeanor. He was dressed like a proper young man, clean with his clothes pressed. He possessed an air of maturity that all in his presence admired. Not many at Otto's age could handle themselves with such poise and keep their wits too. The attorney asked Otto to state his age.

"I am sixteen. I was born in 1886, this month. On the twenty-first I will be seventeen." No sooner had Otto begun his testimony than Judge Thompson adjourned the court; he announced they would reconvene at nine a.m., Thursday, November 5. Otto knew he would be the first witness called; however, for the time being he felt relief in being excused for the day. Stretching his legs was in order. Sitting still for hours on end on hard wooden chairs is hard enough for anyone, but for a sixteen-year old boy, it was undeniably grueling.

Otto and his family took the train from Clarion to Cedar Rapids. They were quiet on the train, watching the scenery blurring by, and listening to the sounds of the steam engine. Sometimes quiet was better than anything else. Sometimes there was not much more that could be spoken. Once in Cedar Rapids, the Ushers retrieved their horses from the livery stable, hitched them to their buggy and were on their way to the one place they could find solace–home. Darkness had already come, accompanied by a chill in the late afternoon air. The Ushers were each thinking what they wanted most at home—a hot meal, a fire, a welcome bed, and the soft glow of the kerosene lamps to light their way to bed. These days the comforts of home were worth more than most anything else. The silence remained as the Ushers ate their dinner. Otto knew Lucy and his father were feeling badly, and he knew, too, they made a conscious decision to keep their feelings to themselves—more than likely to protect Little Walter and himself. There were no sounds but the scraping of plates, and the swallowing of Lucy's delicious meal. Hard to imagine being able to eat at such a time, but the Ushers were learning how life continues even when everything seems stacked dab against you.

# Chapter 30

The Ushers were up early on Thursday morning. No one felt like sleeping in, not even Lucy who had every reason to be fatigued and get some extra rest. The entire Usher family attended court that day, and took seats in the filled courtroom. Interest in the Garrity murder had not abated much to the Usher's dismay. The attorneys and jury members were seated in their usual places as the trial was called to order at nine o'clock.

Otto was recalled to the stand to testify. He felt buffered from a night at home with his family and he was eager to get the testimony over. Assistant Attorney Joe Crosby for the state began the questioning. Otto spoke with courage, and honesty. All present could see the deep love Otto had for his father as he answered the questions put before him. Attorney Crosby was not amiable. Otto thought he was just about the most cantankerous and overbearing fellow he had ever known as he constantly interrupted the boy's responses. While the attorney drilled him, Otto felt he was attempting to get him to change his testimony to fit the attorney's

agenda. Otto tried to be patient. His experience had not prepared him for such an ordeal. At last Otto asked Attorney
Crosby, "Do you just want me to guess the answers to your
questions?"

Judge Thompson threw up his arms. He assured there was
to be no guessing in this court as he threw down his mallet. Attorney Crosby calmed himself down a bit after some
merriment and tranquility permeated the courtroom once
more. It was difficult for the attorney to find the humor in
Otto's statement.

For more than two hours Otto had been on the stand, and
he felt as though he had been through the wringer. His mind
began to drift. He had a hard time staying present in the
courtroom and dwelling on a night he would just as soon
forget. He thought of better things. He had continued to
think of the good times and the hunting he had done this
past summer. In spite of all the farm work and events going
on, he and his friends had had a fun summer.

Otto shook himself back to the present and the tiresome
proceedings as he heard Attorney Crosby speaking yet again.

"The evidence shows that Garrity was unarmed and that
Usher was armed. If the defendant had had longer to think
about it he would have had Garrity armed. You must believe
gentlemen of the jury, that Usher was acting in self-defense
before you can go into the theory. A blow on the head, a
push backward, would have stopped Garrity. If he was coming toward Usher, which we do not believe, the theory of
self-defense was concocted for a purpose."

Commenting on Otto's testimony, Mr. Crosby said,
"Otto's examination was necessarily in the nature of a

cross-examination. He was first on the scene. His testimony was peculiar in many respects, but he wanted naturally to protect his father. And I am willing to extend the cloak of charity. If the homicide was accidental, as they would make you believe, then why did they have the anxiety of burning up the bedding and furniture in that room? We will never be able to tell you, but Usher knows. If Garrity could rise up this morning and tell the truth, you would find that the theory of the state is correct. That William Garrity was lying peaceably on his side when he was shot.

"I believe that we have wrapped a chain of evidence around this defendant. It shows him guilty of this crime of murder in the first degree. Joseph Usher is entitled to the severest penalty in the statute for the punishment of the same."

Otto's heart was breaking for his father at this moment. Joseph was pale and staring down like a beaten man. Otto was accustomed to seeing his father standing tall and proud, meeting the gaze of others directly, not hanging his head in shame. He realized his father barely took in the eager crowd, and when he searched Lucy's face, he could see the sadness and pain etched in such a way it did not seem fleeting, but as if it were there to stay. Lucy had been listening to the testimony without once loosing her focus. She knew she would be called upon soon to testify herself. Otto could see how uncomfortable it was for his stepmother to be sitting so long since she was at the end of her pregnancy. He worried about her comfort and health.

Not until eleven o'clock was Otto finally dismissed with Crosby's closing, and at last Judge Thompson called for a brief recess until one p.m.; the jurors were once again reminded not to discuss the case.

For Otto those two hours were an insufficient break. He would have preferred to never set foot in that courtroom again, but he knew he had to return for the sake of his father and Lucy. After the recess, the state called Fred J. Lazell, City Editor of *The Republican,* as their first witness. Crosby began the questioning.

Mr. Lazell testified: "I have known Joseph Usher for two and a half years. Usher has been delivering milk at my home. I saw him at the police station. I heard his original statement, in which he declared that Garrity had died of hemorrhage of the lungs. I wrote that statement in long hand." He was asked to identify the statement, which he did. "This statement was signed by Usher."

Redmond, for the defense, objected to the introduction of this statement in evidence. However, the court overruled the objection and the statement was read as follows:

"Garrity was at my place since March 12. He worked by the day. Monday night we came home together from town. He did odd jobs, did chores and cut up some stove wood. Was always good friends with him, he never quarreled with me or my wife. I have known him for ten years. We never heard of him being married. Monday evening I returned home about six o'clock. And he had not drunk any. To my knowledge he had no money saved up. He was always asking for money. He helped me milk the cows and do the chores. We had supper about seven o'clock. There were present myself and wife, two boys. one nineteen and one about eight or nine and him—with us there was five people."

Question: "What was done yesterday?"

"He did a few odd jobs and put up a little stove wood. When I returned home he had been milking a little. His health for the past two or three years has not been good. He did not work very hard. I paid him a dollar a day and his board. He worked steady except when he would come to town when he would get pretty full. None of us ever had any trouble with him. We all liked him first rate. When he was not with me I got along without him until he would sober up again. Tuesday night we were all at home. The boy got home from town where he had been with a load of hogs. We all had supper together. He did not eat much, said his stomach wasn't feeling right. I supposed it was from the effects of the liquor. We had supper about seven o'clock, did a few chores. I think we went to bed about nine o'clock. He sleeps upstairs. There are two rooms upstairs. Steps lead from the dining room into his room, not into the boy's room. Our room is downstairs, off the sitting room. The boys went to bed in their room upstairs first. They had to pass through his room. In his room there is a bed and some other furniture. The boys went to bed about half an hour before he did. Then my wife went to bed. We two sat there a while. He went to bed first. He took up a lamp and some water before he went to bed. I think. I believe he came down again. The first noise I heard was something like a groan, and I got right up. I thought at first it was one of the boys sick. The boys were sound asleep. His lantern was burning. None of the doors was locked. We never lock any doors. There was no one around besides us that I know of. I don't know what time it was when I woke up. When I went up his body was lying on the bed. I did not touch him. I called him, but he did not answer. I went downstairs and then I called the boys and sent the oldest boy to Spicer's. I did not touch him, did not notice how his arm lay, but noticed blood in his mouth. Ira Conley came and we sat and waited to hear from the coroner. Conley did not go upstairs. I am not sure about this. I went to telephone to Cedar Rapids. He rang up Gibney and rang up Covington. We have to ring Covington first. None of us touched the body. I did not hear any shot. It sounded more like a groan. The boy has a shotgun, I think. Don't know, maybe the boy had a little bit of a rifle. I am not sure. I don't know whether I ever heard it or not. I think his eyes were open. He did not move or speak. I woke up everyone as quickly as I could. None of us touched the body. We left the lantern burning. I don't know who sent for Courtney Ranck. I wanted Coroner King to see what the trouble was. Ranck was there about eight o'clock. I told them they had better wait till the coroner came. It was my idea he ought to come first before the body was moved. They said there was no use waiting. I supposed he was dead when I went downstairs. I was frightened. I am nervous and easily get frightened and worried when anything goes wrong around the place. The day before Garrity had complained about not feeling well. He had said he would come down town Wednesday and get some medicine. I don't know where the rifle was kept. I don't pay any attention to such things. I don't remember ever having seen him have it. I don't know how he died except what I have told. The undertaker called it a hemorrhage of the lungs. I suppose that is what he died from. I don't know. I'm no doctor. I don't think anyone of us heard a rifle shot that night. I don't know. Nobody said anything about a shot. There was a shotgun and a rifle. I don't know where they were kept.

I told Spicer's folks they might as well burn up all the things in the room. They were going up there to help clean up. I don't know whether it was an iron bedstead or a wooden one. I have lived on the place about twenty-five years. I have been married twice. My second marriage was about three years ago to a woman named Gillis. I own the hundred on which I live, but owe some on it yet. We never lock our doors. It would be possible for someone to go through our house. And up to his room without waking us up. I never quarreled with Garrity, never heard of his having trouble with anyone around here. I don't know if he had liquor on the place Tuesday. Sometimes he had some. I thought Garrity's breath smelled some Tuesday night and thought that he talked off a little bit. I wouldn't have let him have whisky if I had known it."

Question: "When did you first hear this man was shot?"

"Right here, right now."

Question: "Don't you know that you are the man that fired that shot?"

"No, I am not. I didn't shoot him. I didn't know he was shot. I never had any trouble with him. I didn't know he was shot until just now. I didn't order his clothes burned because I wanted to destroy the evidence. I thought it would be easier than to wash them. I went down to Spicer's and asked them to come out and help clean up a little. I told them they might as well burn up those things. I did not order them to burn up his everyday clothes; only the bed. I wasn't jealous of this man and my wife. I never had any occasion. I am not of a jealous disposition. My boy never had any trouble with him. I know my boy had a rifle but didn't know where he got it or where he kept it. I don't know how it came to be in the oats bin. I have to be away on the milk rout, Sundays and all. My boy has been married but his wife got a bill of divorce. I think he is about 17 years old. One of my children is married to P.J. Dudley, Norman Avenue, Chicago. I have another son married, living in Chickasaw county. I had no trouble to speak of with my son and son's wife when they were living together."

(Signed) "JOSEPH A. USHER."

# Chapter 31

Later on the afternoon of Thursday, November 5, W.E. Holmes, City Editor of *The Gazette*, was called to the stand by the state of Iowa. The day seemed interminably long to Joseph, and hearing the recounting of the tragic night one more time made the old expression, rubbing salt in the wound, seem tame. Joseph was practicing the art of being physically present but mentally absent. He was getting skilled at this survival tool, and the beauty of it was, no one seemed to notice but his own family members.

Mr. Holmes testified: "The second statement offered in evidence by the state the transcript of shorthand notes made of Mr. Usher's version of the tragedy is correct." Therefore, the statement was accepted as an exhibit since both sides of the counsel were in agreement. He read the statement Joseph had given about shooting William Garrity in self-defense.

Captain Joseph Kroulik of the Cedar Rapids' Police was summoned to the stand. Joseph tuned out as he spoke crisply, in clipped and terse police fashion. He said nothing new that Joseph could discern but stated, "I did not hear the statement made by the defendant in the evening." And on cross-examination the Captain said, "Usher stated the window was closed. Usher said his wife must have closed it earlier in the evening."

Deputy Marshal Thomas Brown went to the stand following the Captain. Joseph watched the two uniformed men pass one another in the courtroom and felt insufferable fatigue envelope him.

"I know the defendant and I knew Garrity in his lifetime. I saw Usher at the police station on the afternoon of May 27. When he was asked the cause of Garrity's death, he said he had died of a hemorrhage, and that he had nothing to do with it. Later the defendant said that he had shot Garrity." Deputy Brown detailed the conversation previously related by Marshal Kozlovsky, just as his Captain had, all rehashed testimony, and then he emphasized the fact that Usher claimed Garrity was in the act of rising up in the bed when he shot. Cross-examination uncovered nothing new and the witness was excused.

Thomas Gibney was recalled to the stand and said: "When I went to Usher's at six-thirty in the morning of May 27, Usher was hitching up to go to town. Coroner King had been notified and was coming out. I suggested that Usher had better not go away until Mr. King arrived. Usher told his son to put the horses up," and then the witness was dismissed.

Joseph watched as his neighbor, Ed M. Donahue was sworn in and testified: "I have lived in Clinton Township since 1870. I have known Usher for thirty years. He lives a mile north and half a mile west. I saw Usher on May 27, 1903 on First Street. I had a talk with him. Usher stated that

Garrity had but little wages coming to him. I suggested that they ought to take up a collection to defray the funeral expenses. Usher offered to head it with five dollars. Usher did not say anything about Garrity having died from a gunshot wound."

Coroner King was then recalled. He testified: "I saw Usher on First Street, near the Temple. It was about four o'clock in the afternoon of May 27. I saw him later at the police station and heard him make a statement. I had told Usher in the morning that I, was the County Coroner."

On cross-examination the witness stated: "When I first saw the defendant he was on First Street. He was standing on the wheel of a wagon talking to a man I did not know. When Usher left his own team he started in the general direction of the police station. Usher was about twenty or thirty feet from the wagon when arrested."

Even the Judge was looking weary at this point, late in the afternoon, the sun's light pulling back from the courtroom. Court was adjourned until the next morning at nine a.m. Joseph Usher and his family had survived four days of testimony though it may have well been a year. They left the courtroom and headed home with somber faces and deflated posture. They left in silence, as if they were filing out of a funeral.

# Chapter 32

Friday morning, November 6, Judge Thompson called the court to order at nine a.m. This marked the fifth day of Joseph Usher's trial for murder. The Ushers had awoken when the sky was still dark, done their morning chores, and readied themselves for another grueling day. The proceedings from the day before had taken an incredible toll on them all. Joseph had dark circles beneath his eyes that no amount of sleep could fade. Although Lucy was big with child, her face had the appearance of being gaunt and pale, not the robust look of being pregnant. And the boys were not their usual spirited selves. There were no sounds of banter or brotherly jest under the farmhouse roof.

Assistant County Attorney Joe Crosby called Ira J. Conley to the stand as the first witness for the state.

He said, "It was Thomas Gibney who first suggested that Usher, Gibney and I go upstairs. We went upstairs to look at Garrity's body."

Following his statements, Mr. Gibney was also recalled and testified: "When I went to Garrity's room I saw no blood on the bed except at the head."

After Mr. Gibney's brief testimony, Mekota stood and made the announcement that the state would rest. Major Smith, Attorney for the Defense, stood at this moment and recalled Otto on cross-examination. Smith questioned the boy concerning his conversation with his father on May 26th.

Otto said, "Father stated that when he talked with Garrity on the evening of May 26, Garrity talked about 'seeing things in the air,' and also something on a tree. Father went over and pulled it off. It proved to be a knot."

On re-direct examination Otto stated: "I was at Mr. Redmond's office last night. We discussed the line of testimony I was to give on cross-examination this morning."

Questions as to whether it was planned to booster up the opening statement for counsel of the defense were overruled by the court.

Otto said, "The night Garrity was alleged to have 'seen things' he had milked several cows. He had been working all day about the place." Otto was dismissed.

Redmond opened for the defense, and the first witness he called was William Sutliff. In addition, those witnesses for the defense who were present were then sworn in by the court. There were fifteen witnesses in all.

Redmond questioned Mr. Sutliff, who responded, "I am a farmer. I have lived in Clinton Township for thirty years. I knew William Garrity. I know he has been addicted to drink for three or four years. He complained to me a good deal concerning his health and said he was under the doctor's care."

George Usher of Chickasaw County, son of Joseph Usher, was the second witness for the defense, and he said, "I made my home on my father's farm until March 3, 1903. I have never seen my father handle a firearm. I knew Garrity. He told me last fall that he wasn't feeling well. He claimed to have contracted a loathsome disease. I knew he was addicted to drink."

On cross-examination George Usher said, "I last saw Garrity in the latter part of February. I have an old shotgun at home. Father had cautioned me about handling it."

Mr. Dickinson was called to the stand next; it was mid-morning and most people in the courtroom were getting antsy, in need of stretching their legs and getting up from the hard wooden chairs. "I met Garrity in a saloon on F Avenue West in Cedar Rapids. It was the Monday before his death. I asked him to have a glass of beer. He said he would rather have whisky."

The next to testify was Captain Mike McGuire of the Cedar Rapids Police Force. "I knew Garrity. I have noticed him often, and he was drunk every time I saw him. He was arrested at times and turned out when sobered up." Captain McGuire reported that Garrity was drunk as late as April, 1903 and stated: "Usher's character for peaceable behavior around Cedar Rapids was good."

Captain Charles McKernan was the next witness. He testified: "I have seen Garrity brought into the station in an intoxicated condition several times." Captain McKernan could not say how many times Garrity had been convicted. On cross-examination the captain said, "I never knew him to have delirium tremors." On re-direct examination he said, "Usher's character for peacefulness prior to May 26, 1903 was good."

The Defense called William Langham. "I have lived in Clinton Township forty years. I know Joseph Usher and have for many years. His character as a peaceable citizen prior to May 26, 1903 was good."

When called to the stand by the Defense, W.F. Donman stated, "I formerly resided in Clinton Township. I knew Joseph Usher for twenty-seven years. His character for peacefulness prior to May 26, 1903 was good."

William Howard testified for the Defense. "I formerly farmed in Clinton Township. I knew Joseph Usher from the cradle up and his character for peacefulness is good." On cross-examination Mr. Howard stated, "I was an Officer of the United Building Company." The questions as to the standing of the company were ruled out. He stated, "I am one of Usher's bondsmen."

When Cyrus Upton of Cedar Rapids was called he said, "I have resided in Cedar Rapids for forty years. Usher's character for peacefulness prior to May 26, 1903 was good."

Attorney Redmond was satisfied with his character witnesses so far and took his seat.

At this time Defense Attorney Smith called Coroner King to the stand. He began the examination.

Coroner King testified: "I conducted the inquest over Garrity's body on May 28. Mr. Ranck was one of the witnesses. I was a witness before Justice Rail in the preliminary examination. I heard Ranck ask whether Usher wanted him to make haste in taking Garrity's body away. He replied that Usher wanted him to wait until the coroner and a neighbor came. Ranck so testified."

Miss Alice M. Hall was the next witness to be called to the stand and reported the evidence in the preliminary hearing.

She testified: "Ranck was a witness in that hearing. When Ranck testified he was a witness before the coroner's jury. His testimony before that body was correct so far as I knew."

Portions of her transcript of that evidence were offered in evidence by the defense.

J.S Taylor of Covington was called. He testified: "I saw Garrity in Cedar Rapids on May 20, 1903. He was under the influence of liquor." On the cross-examination the witness said, "I have known Garrity for three or four years. But I had never seen him drunk but the one time."

The next witness called was W.L. Sleight of Cedar Rapids. He testified: "I knew Garrity in his lifetime and I saw him in an intoxicated condition on May 20, 1903." On cross-examination witness stated, "Garrity was quiet and not quarrelsome."

Judge Thompson announced that the next witness would be the last one before the noon break.

There was a collective sigh in the courtroom as people looked forward to the break, and as the testimonies had been rather uneventful.

Wes Weubgartl was then called. He was a west side saloon man. He testified: "I knew Garrity. He had been drinking a little. Garrity had never bought anything to drink in my place."

Judge Thompson adjourned the court at eleven forty-five until one p.m.

Dinner once more was brought in to the court for Joseph. The Ushers stayed close and tried to relax. Otto spoke a great deal, with nervous energy, trying to distract his pained father and Lucy. The time passed quickly and before they realized it was already approaching one in the afternoon, with everybody taking their places in the crowded courtroom.

Judge Thompson called the court to order and the crowd became quiet with the awed respect a man presiding over a legal case garners.

Once the afternoon session began Mrs. Jennie Dudley of Chicago, daughter of Joseph Usher, was called to testify–along with William Usher of Chickasaw County, a half-brother, Henry Usher, a distant cousin, Justice J.F. Rail, John McAllister of Palo, and L.G, Wilson of Cedar Rapids, a hostler in a livery stable.

The witnesses called were examined until two o'clock, providing nothing new in the way of evidence. Lucy squirmed in her seat. She knew her time to testify was next, and due to nerves, she had eaten nothing over the break. Joseph had nudged a piece of bread with butter into her hands, but she couldn't nibble even the smallest bit. Instead she drank some water and felt the waves of unease slosh about inside of her. She was lightheaded but now that the time had arrived, Lucy had regained strength enough to take the stand for the sake of her husband and family.

Smith called Joseph's wife to the stand. The crowd felt extreme pity for Lucy as she walked slowly and took the seat she had dreaded. She had watched Otto testify and thought she had to be more brave more poised than he had been. Lucy had never heard such silence as she sat waiting to speak. She looked at the clock and saw it was ten minutes after two. The hands of the clock seemed frozen. Joseph gave Lucy a loving glance, and tried to impart his strength to her.

"I was at home when Ranck came to take Garrity's body away. I heard my husband say not to take it. I remember sitting on the porch the night before and heard Garrity say something. He was talking about somebody saying something about him at the Arcade Hotel. I have gotten off a sick bed to come to court."

Lucy was not subjected to any cross-examination. Even though all eyes were still on her, and she felt self-conscious, taking leave of the stand felt like a relief she had never before known. Her baby gave a tremendous kick, as if knowing there was something to celebrate. Lucy was proud of herself for having kept her composure, for not losing her voice, for not breaking into a sob. Her neighbors eyed her with kindness, and for this, too, she was entirely grateful.

Sometimes in the darkness of night, when problems always had a way of seeming worse, Lucy believed she and Joseph had become pariahs in their community. She shuddered as she reflected on the sordid affair between Hulda and Joseph, and add to that the disgrace of Garrity's murder; it was too much to bear. But seeing all the looks of concern and warmth, on this day in particular, gave Lucy the ability to go on, and she had to go on—she was with child and Little Walter and Otto relied upon her too.

Smith called Constable O.C. Carpenter, who testified: "I have known the defendant twenty odd years. I am in the sewing machine business. Usher is a nervous, excitable man."

The defense then called Dr. George Carpenter and Dr. Arthur Hamilton of Independence as expert witnesses. After their testimonies the two witnesses were dismissed.

By now it was late Friday afternoon and Judge Thompson adjourned the court for the day. He stated that the court would resume the trial of Joseph Usher on Monday November 9, 1903, and again the juror's were given instruction not to discuss the case.

Daylight had not yet left as the Usher's journeyed home. The evening was cool, and the setting sun illuminated the autumn leaves, making the oranges, reds and yellows even more brilliant. Lucy took Joseph's hand. Under different circumstances this would have been a romantic drive home, the sound of the horses feet clomping on the hardened dirt road, and the smell of neighbor's fires burning as they passed by warmly lit houses, where families without such dire woes were preparing dinner and conversing about their days.

Lucy took a deep breath. Today would be the last day of the trial she would be able to attend. Her body was not able to bear any more stress of travel. She needed bed rest as much as she longed to be present for Joseph's sake. She had their baby to think of, and the weekend was filled with preparing for the birth. A handmade cradle was brought in from the shed and cleaned up. The last this cradle had been used was for Little Walter. Lucy smiled at Walter as she tried to imagine him fitting inside the small infant bed. He was growing taller, and was her helper, being accommodating with whatever her needs were.

A midwife was secured to come and assist Lucy with the delivery of her baby. Joseph was concerned for Lucy's health, and because of the experience he had with his first wife giving birth, he knew what lay ahead. He made plans for Lucy not to be alone at all the next week, and she appreciated his attentiveness and protectiveness.

Fall was late this year and this was a blessing, for even though frost has come a couple of nights, so far there had been not so much as a dusting of snow. The wood stove helped stave off whatever mild chill was in the air, and the men made sure to keep it stoked. The Ushers sat before the blazing fire. No one recounted the day in court. This was not necessary. Instead, they sat watching the flames cast glowing shadows on the walls of their farmhouse, each family member lost in his or her own thoughts. Otto wished he still had his guns so he could be going hunting with his friends this Sunday. Joseph sat, terrified, wondering if his days in this home with his loved ones were numbered. The anticipation of the unknown was hanging over the Ushers like a menacing storm that turns the sky some ungodly shade of green, and threatens a tornado, or some strong hurricane, stealing the home right out from under your feet.

# Chapter 33

Monday, November 9, came far too quickly for Joseph. He took leave of his wife early in the morning and rode away from their warm farmhouse, feeling a pull to stay. Of all times to have to be leaving his wife, and for what? A criminal trial that would decide his fate and the fate of his family.

The courtroom had not lost its fill of spectators.

Judge Thompson called the trial to order promptly at nine a.m. and despite the packed room, all in attendance were respectfully silent as another day of purgatory began for Joseph Usher.

Redmond stood in front of the court and took up the closing argument for the defense.

First he addressed the purpose of criminal law: "It has been said that it is better for a thousand guilty men to escape than to punish an innocent one. Mr. Crosby's review of the evidence had been fair, in the main. The jury cannot go into the field of imagination to find a motive. But the juror's must decide upon the evidence alone. The evidence is manifestly overdrawn and crippled on behalf of the state. Men do not commit crimes without motive.

"The state confessed to you that it has no evidence to establish a motive. It is enough to establish a reasonable doubt that Joseph Usher did not commit this crime. Nobody ever knew him to have a quarrel with William Garrity, or anybody else. The state confesses it. That corroborates just what Joseph Usher said. His statement of how the unfortunate thing happened. There is no reason assigned why Usher should commit that crime. When Usher held up his hand before the coroner he told the truth.

"The state says it has its theories. But it cannot ask you to find a man guilty of such a crime on imaginary theories. The state takes the position that because Usher did not tell the truth that night, or in the early morning, that his story isn't true and that he is guilty of murder. They argue that Usher wanted to destroy all evidence of his crime by burning the things in the room, and that isn't true. They argue that they wanted to get Garrity out of the way by calling the township trustees. But that isn't true."

Redmond stated emphatically that the theory of the defense was not built up as charged by the state. He said: "William Garrity was a man forty-three years of age, unmarried, with no family. He worked about the county for the neighbors, by the day. He had not worked for his relative, Mr. Gibney."

Redmond referred to the matter of the disease the defense claimed Garrity was suffering from by stating: "It was only important in one point."

"He went on to say that Garrity was arrested for drunkenness in Cedar Rapids in April. On the fifteenth of May he left

Usher's and went to town to go to the circus. He remained some days and was intoxicated most of the time. Otto told him when he left to take care of himself. Garrity told him he was going to get a gun and fix McGuire if he bothered him. Garrity was intoxicated on May 20, and was fired out of the livery barn. Two men who went to school with him testified that they saw him intoxicated. Mr. Chambers found him drunk in a water closet. Mr. Dickinson says that Garrity was drinking.

"The state puts on a saloon-keeper that says Garrity was not drinking. That he took a glass of seltzer. It is one of the things that a drinking man thinks about. It was something to use to tone up his stomach and steady his nerves. Yet Chambers says Garrity drank with him on Saturday. Mr. Dickinson bought whisky for him on Monday. They were bosom friends of Garrity.

"Mr. Dickinson and Garrity went out into the street. He loaned Garrity fifty cents. Then Garrity asked him. 'Who are those men? Are they after me?' Mr. Dickinson said he could see no one. We have shown through his testimony that Garrity was already 'seeing things,' before Joseph Usher came along to take him home. He had done it hundreds of times. They went to work. There wasn't much to do. But the idea was that Garrity would be there when the weather cleared. Then on the porch that evening he asked if Mr. Usher had heard anything about him when he was at the Arcade Hotel. They retired that night as usual.

"The next morning they milked the cows and Usher started for town. The boy took a load of hogs away. When Usher got home he found Garrity talking odd. He thought he was out of his head. The boys tell you what they were talking about."

As Redmond spoke he looked directly at the jury and they paid close attention. This murder trial had managed to keep the interest of the community throughout its duration. The attorney continued his argument by saying, "Usher evolved this defense, a man crude and unschooled in the law, evolved this defense in his statement at the police station before the officials and reporters. Now, is it true or untrue? Could he have told a story that would have been corroborated from every point of view? Not unless the story had been true."

Referring to the details of Usher's statement about Garrity "seeing things," Attorney Redmond said: "Counsel for the defense did not know the details of the alleged conversation. Until the details were brought out by the state. It had been shown that Garrity was sick. They were going to town the next day for medicine."

On the events of the fatal night, Redmond recalled the fact that Garrity asked Otto if they could hang a man for saying something about somebody.

"He asked for the gun.

"Later Garrity and Usher looked at the paper and laughed at a picture. Mrs. Usher and Walter retired, and then Garrity asked for the lantern. Why? Because he was afraid. He took the water because he did not feel well."

Commenting on the cleaning up of the room, Redmond said, "He went and asked the neighbors to do it. He didn't want his wife to handle the things. No evidence was destroyed. The bullet was in the body of the man. The neighbors saw all the evidence before the body was taken away.

So did Mr. Ranck. But none of them make it appear that any evidence was destroyed. This is the first time in my experience that I have ever heard a judge warn a public prosecutor that he was making a mistake in the handling of a case.

"In my judgment Usher had to be hounded. And his wife dragged off a sickbed to make out the shadow of a case. Usher was not going away when Gibney had advised him to wait until the coroner came. Mr. Gibney has made two or three different statements. If Cordy Ranck had had the conscience of a chipmunk he would have waited until the coroner had come. There never would have been a prosecution. The statement of Mr. Gibney that Usher wanted the trustees—it was made for the first time on the witness stand.

"Usher knew the coroner was coming, and so did Ranck. He wanted to get the body away for fear he might lose a case. Before Justice Rall, Mr. Ranck swore that Usher asked him to wait until the coroner came. Mr. Gibney himself was finally driven to say that Usher was waiting for the coroner. He was not waiting for Ranck. Usher was long due in Cedar Rapids with his milk. Gibney told him the coroner was coming. Usher put his horses back in the barn. Usher had about given up the idea that Mr. King was coming.

"Ranck started out and met the coroner, who was angry. The coroner told Ranck that he ought to have left the body there. There was some talk with Usher later. Joseph Usher never knew the words 'hemorrhage of the lungs,' until Spicer asked him if Garrity had not died from hemorrhage? Ranck mentioned it later. Usher knew from King's conversation that there would be an inquest. He was then two hours late for his usual rounds. He went down and attempted to run his milk route. When he was through he tied his team. He talked with Donahue, who asked if Garrity had any money coming to him.

"Then Donahue suggested that they make up a purse to bury him. Usher said, 'I'll give five dollars to it.' There wasn't a syllable as to the cause of Garrity's death. Then what happened? Mr. Usher was going in the direction of the official center of the city. He met Marshal Kozlovsky. He had concluded his work and was worried. He didn't know the gun had been found or that there had been an autopsy. It may have been running through his mind to find a lawyer. I don't know. He would expect in his ignorance to find the coroner at the city hall.

"The state will say if he was waiting for the coroner, why didn't he tell his story straight when arrested and when the coroner was there? Usher did not know Coroner King with his hat off. Supposed he and the county attorney were city officials. If Usher was not dazed he would not have signed a statement saying that Otto took a load of hogs out home that afternoon."

Mr. Redmond then took up the first statement:

"I do not believe Usher remembered that he had signed it. The two statements agree in all details. Except the one detail that he shot Garrity. At the time Usher went into the room to make the second statement, he did not recognize any of the officials. It was necessary for the marshal to introduce him. If Joseph Usher and Otto Usher's statements are true, and this defendant did rub Garrity's feet after he and his son went to Garrity's bedside—it was a natural thing for him to have laid them straight on the bed. Regardless of the position they were found in.

"If Ranck had waited for the arrival of Coroner King before removing Garrity's body, the objects in the room would not have been burned. The facts would have been investigated and published. There probably never would have been an investigation. Usher did not order the bedding burned because it would destroy any evidence. It was easier to burn than to wash it. He only ordered the bedding burned, not Garrity's clothing."

Reviewing the second statement made by Mr. Usher, and which was taken in shorthand, Mr. Redmond pointed out, "Although Usher asked if he could have an attorney, the marshal did not get one for him. He knew that a lawyer would have asked for a private consultation. A lawyer would have advised him to say nothing at that time. His idea of getting those other gentlemen in was the responsibility of the police force. At that time he thought Garrity was out of his head. This has been the theory of the defense since that time."

Redmond recalled the fact that Usher claimed then that Garrity was "acting odd."

However, officials had not interrogated him in detail as to how Garrity had acted. Attorney Redmond affirmed that. "At that time Usher stated Garrity was his friend. If Usher had been trying to patch up a story he could have claimed the contrary. The testimony has corroborated and amplified it. That statement was the God's truth, and nothing has occurred to contradict it. The state has nothing except the fact that Usher did not tell the truth the first time. The state has nothing to ask or expect a conviction on. Every part of that statement is true, and you must consider it all together. I believe Joseph Usher is innocent of murder."

He cautioned the jury about reading the papers. "The press cannot," he said, "for obvious reasons, take the side opposite the state in such cases. I admit that Usher has not told the truth in his first statement. I believe the jury can understand the reason. Therefore in what has been brought out in evidence, the state can search Clinton Township with a fine-toothed comb without finding a man who would say Joseph Usher has ever been anything but a peaceful citizen."

In closing he said, "I have heard Joseph Usher's statement and I don't believe he is guilty. I know he is not. A man who has lived and worked as he has does not turn out to be a murderer. Not in a single night. William Garrity squandered his substance in licentiousness. He drank life to the dregs. All the retribution that should have been his has settled down on Joseph Usher. If Garrity could break the bonds of the grave he would come up here this afternoon and give the lie to the gentlemen across the table."

Redmond closed with a magnificent appeal to the jury for the acquittal of his client. There were tears in many eyes and great emotion filled the room. Following his closing, the attorney took his seat.

Defense Attorney Smith then took the floor at three-thirty, p.m. In opening his address he said, "There is nothing for me to do but to rake after the wagon. Mr. Redmond has covered everything in the most exhaustive manner. The court would give the jury the interpretations of several points of law in his instructions, one of them being that a man has the right to protect himself. It originates in the human heart. If serious consequences result, the man who acts in self-defense is not responsible therefore. There is another principle of law—that before a man shall be sentenced or incarcerated for a crime, it must be proven beyond a reasonable doubt that he did commit a crime—that he was not acting in self-defense. It is also the law that a man's good reputation can be brought up to sustain him in his hour of need."

Smith added, "If the state succeeds in the prosecution, it must succeed upon the specific charge in the indictment. That of murder in the first degree—or the defendant must be acquitted. The jury must conclude that Usher deliberately planned the death of Garrity, or that Garrity died as Usher said in that last statement. Did he plan it? Is the first of these propositions true? While the court will tell you that it is not necessary in a case like this to prove a motive, every man has a motive in his heart. If he was out of his head, he is not responsible. If he is in his sane mind and does it in self-defense, he is not responsible.

"If a man commits murder it is through a desire for gain or for revenge. In my twelve years experience as a public prosecutor, I have prosecuted over twenty-five people on the charge of murder. I cannot recall a case where the motive was not apparent at some stage of the proceedings. No man is satisfied in his own heart to say that 'A' killed 'B', unless he knew there was a motive for it. The first inquiry in cases of that kind is 'why?' What in the world did he kill him for?

"That's the question people would ask if the report were to go out that Joseph Mekota had killed Major Smith. Did Joseph Usher have any motive to kill William Garrity? No, Garrity liked to stay at Usher's. He had made it his home there. The record is just as bare of evidence as to any trouble between those men. As bare as this floor is of green grass.

Usher had lived in Clinton Township all his life. He belongs to a family that all old settlers remember. He is a timorous man, kind and affectionate. He is a remarkably industrious man. He never had a lawsuit or a quarrel; he's the sort of man you would associate with if he lived in your neighborhood.

"Garrity was in one sense a good man. But unfortunately for him, he was addicted to too much drink. If it had not been for the grog shop, we never would have had this trial. The habit of drinking took possession of him. The poor fellow is to be pitied and not blamed. We have these two men, the employer and the hired man. Bill, when he was in town was waiting for the 'old man.' That is a term of endearment for Garrity. Everything was just as peaceable between those men as it is between the present counsel for the state.

"Joseph Usher never got that gun, loaded it and snuffed out the life of Garrity, unless he thought Garrity had done something against him. You have got to believe that he deliberately planned and executed that crime if you believe the theory of the state. There isn't a thing except some of the first statements he made contradicting our theory. If he had not killed William Garrity except in self-defense, why did he not leave the gun there and give it out that it was suicide? The doctors, Carpenter and Hamilton, said that when a man is just getting over a debauch, his nerves are unstrung and that he is apt to act just as Garrity did. When he has alcoholic insanity he has imaginary enemies. He sees things in the air. When these paroxysms come on he is liable to act dangerously."

Smith then cited several cases within his own experience and acquaintance, where men suffering from alcoholism

185

had tried to get weapons, and restraint had prevented tragedies.

He recalled Garrity's remarks to Mr. Dickinson about the men he thought were following him and his references to the alleged foes and objects at the Usher place.

Smith said, "These are the very marks of alcoholism and conform to the conditions the doctors say indicate alcoholic insanity, as does his unusual request. Garrity asked permission to take a light up to bed with him. The father, who after a hard day's work gets up, goes to look after a sick son is not the kind to commit a murder. Joseph Usher heard a noise and went upstairs in his drawers and shirt. Murderers don't do that.

"He stepped to the window. Right behind him was a maniac, who had seen visions. He had heard noises, and was in a condition when he didn't know friend from foe. He easily imagined when he saw Mr. Usher at the window—'There's the man that is after me,' and sprang out of bed. Usher saw the glare of the maniac in his eyes. He called Usher's attention to the gun; he grabbed it and shot. Do you blame him? When a man stands in the presence of apparent death he may do the thing that he thinks is proper."

Smith cited the attempted killing of Judge Fields of California by Judge Ferry. When a detective shot the latter dead, the courts acquitted him. "The law says one may defend others as well as himself from impending danger.

"If Usher had not seen that gun there would have been no trial. There would have been a funeral for Joseph Usher. Poor Bill Garrity would have been sent to the insane asylum."

Smith recalled the assassinations of Garfield, Mayor Harrison, and McKinley. And the fact the people inquired why someone had not killed the assassins. The assassins had gotten away from the scenes of their acts. The jurors and the crowd listened intently. It was getting late on Monday afternoon and he continued with his summary of the trial.

"There is something in the human heart," he said, "that tells a man that he has a right to protect himself in the presence of imminent danger, even to the taking of life, and this is also the law. A man is not required to exercise the coolest judgment. Or take the course he would otherwise have taken."

At this time Judge Thompson interrupted, since it was past the time to adjourn for the afternoon session. Smith would complete his statement to the jury tomorrow morning at nine a.m. on Tuesday, November 10, 1903. The jury was excused for the afternoon with the usual instructions.

The courtroom was full of spectators even at this late hour. When the room was adjourned you could hear the crowd. They began to express their feelings about the day's proceedings. This was turning out to be the most remarkable murder trial in the history of Linn County.

Joseph's counsel was feeling confident. They had done a good job presenting their case in his defense.

On Tuesday morning, November 10, 1903, the closing moments of the trial attracted a large audience. Those present were many of the relatives of the defendant and the deceased.

There were people from Cedar Rapids and Marion, a large number of which were ladies. After Judge Thompson called the court to order, Smith resumed his argument for the defense.

"The County Attorney might claim there was no evidence from alcoholic insanity. He might claim that there was no evidence of that fact. He might claim that the autopsy did not show any signs of disease caused by alcohol. But the facts were there may have been such evidence. The defense had no physician present when the autopsy was made. Only the Doctor's, King and Johnson, were there. They made an examination of the course of the ball. That was all. They made no examination of the stomach, or the liver, or the heart. They were not thinking of it. They were thinking only of the course of the ball. Had they examined the brain or the heart, or the stomach for traces of alcoholism they might have found them."

He continued, "I have no doubt that Garrity had gone upstairs that night with the intention of getting that rifle. He wanted the lantern to see to get the cartridges and load the rifle. He walked around Otto's bed, took down the rifle, got the cartridges. He loaded the rifle and laid it near the head of the bed. It was as far from the stairway as possible when Usher walked passed his bed and started to close the window. Garrity, his mind filled with the thoughts of his imaginary foes. He imagined that Usher was one of them, coming after him. It was then that he sprang out of bed to get the rifle to defend himself. When Gibney and the rest of the state's witnesses saw Garrity, he appeared to be in his usual health. That was no proof that he was not suffering from alcohol dementia. That disease comes on in paroxysms. At times the patient is lucid, at other moments he is in a frenzy of fear."

Smith said, "I desire the jury, in their minds, to press the county attorney hard for a motive which might have prompted such a crime. There was no motive. No motive of gain, of jealousy, of intimacy with his wife, or of personal ill-feeling. No motive whatever."

As the last of his illustrations to defend Usher, Attorney Smith referred to the Bible. "It was Moses who slew the Egyptian, who was killing an Israelite. He hid the Egyptian in the sand, looked this way and that, and fled. God said it was all right, didn't punish him for it. But God made him the chosen leader of his people. Usher's previous good character for peacefulness must weigh in his favor against which the state has offered no evidence."

With this closing statement Major Smith rested and resumed his seat. Joseph Usher and Attorney Smith exchanged glances: the look between them was one of confidence and hope, but inside the defendant was feeling anything but these emotions.

# Chapter 34

B y nine-thirty, Mekota stood in front of the courtroom with all the expectant jurors, as well as Joseph Usher, his anxious family and the equally anxious family of William Garrity—who awaited justice for the murder of their loved one. Attorney Mekota took a deep breath, knowing what was at stake, and began:–"It is not incumbent on the state to show a motive for the crime or what was in Joseph Usher's mind. In the greater majority of cases, the motive–no matter what it is–there is no excuse for the fact. The fact is, William Garrity was killed and Joseph Usher did the killing. No crime is logical or reasonable, and there can be no excuse. Therefore, the man who commits murder generally blunders. Thereafter, and the present case is no exception. If Garrity had attacked Usher the picture would have been so indefeasibly fixed on his mind. The story would have been the first thing to come to his mind. No man would have failed to tell the truth at once if he had been innocent. In which point the defendant failed, according to the admissions of his own counsel. When a man starts out to lie about things, he is sure to get tripped up. That was when Usher began to blunder. If he was innocent there was no occasion for him to tell what he did. Or to hide the gun, or to burn the things in Garrity's room. He lied straight through to everybody."

Mekota paused, scrutinized the jurors and said, "The only pain I have experienced in the case was when Mr. Redmond accused the state of being unfair. The defense has had every scrap of evidence in the knowledge of the state. There can be no room for the charge of unfairness."

The County Attorney then addressed the charge that the case had been forced to trial. "In my opinion, five and a half months was efficient time for the defense to prepare."

Then commenting on Otto Usher's statement, he said, "I have the greatest sympathy for the boy. While I believe, he would have testified differently had it not been for his sense of devotion to his father. Usher never suspected that the coroner would hold an inquest. He thought Mr. King would believe him, as his neighbors had. That Garrity had died of hemorrhage. Why didn't he tell the truth to Mr. King? When he met that official in the road with Mr. Gibney?"

Mekota commented upon the claim of the defense that no evidence had been destroyed in the Usher home. "When the things in Garrity's room were burned, if Garrity had been killed three or four feet from the bed– the carpet would have told. Had he been shot in bed, some bullet holes might have been found in the bedding.

"I do not believe that C.H. Ranck deserves the criticism that the defense has heaped upon him. Usher's first answer to Ranck's question was that it was not murder. He said that Garrity had died from natural causes. Usher could have prevented the removal of the body if he had wanted to. But he didn't want to."

Mekota searched the faces in the courtroom to make sure that his closing statement was being followed, then he proceeded to review the defendant's statement of the shooting.

"Why did Usher go into Garrity's room first, when, according to his own version of the affair, he had gone upstairs for the express purpose of looking after his son who was sleeping in the adjoining room? In Usher's first statement he claimed Garrity was 'raising on the bed,' not that he was out on the floor. Usher did not say then that Garrity was a maniac. Usher must have been some feet away from Garrity when he shot. If Mr. Redmond's theory is correct, the two men were in striking distance. Garrity's shirt would have shown some powder marks, but it does not. If Garrity had been insane and believed that he was being pursued by imaginary foes and objects, would it not have taken more than one cartridge? Would he not have taken the shotgun and all the ammunition? Would Garrity not have taken the rifle to bed or set it within easy reach? Instead Garrity put the gun at the further side of the room. Bill Garrity did not whisper the words attributed to him by the defense. 'Damn you–I'm going to kill you.' If he said them Otto would have heard them in the next room. Usher did not need to shoot Garrity. The gun was at no time in Garrity's possession. The defense claims Usher's first thought was of Garrity's alleged insane conduct on the night before. Yet he did not think of calling Otto, who slept only ten feet away."

In referring to the testimony of the physicians, the County Attorney said: "It all corroborates the claim of the state that

Garrity was shot. As he was lying on his side, or as he was rising from the bed. It is also corroborated by the testimony of Gibney and Conley on the condition of the body. There is the fact that there was no blood on the bed. The only blood was on the pillow immediately about the head."

Mekota commented that he felt Mrs. Usher's testimony was not relevant in any regard: "I do not understand why counsel for the defense had deemed it necessary. They did not need to bring Mrs. Usher off a sick bed to give that sort of evidence."

Next he examined the evidence concerning Garrity's condition during the several days prior to his death. "There was absolutely nothing, except the statements of the Ushers and Mr. Dickinson. There is nothing to show that Garrity was on the verge of alcoholic insanity. Several reputable citizens testified to having observed Garrity's actions up to the night of his death. None of them noticed the first indication of mental unbalance.

"I will not attempt to tell you jurors any stories, such as the stories Major Smith told. But I desire to call attention to the three cases cited by Mr. Smith. Which are the murders of Garfield, Harrison and McKinley. And, to the fact, in each case the murderer had admitted his guilt and pleaded insanity. The law requires the prosecution of persons upon who rests the suspicion of a crime, and in this case I have only done my duty. It is in the firm belief that Joseph Usher is guilty. It is not necessary for a man to premeditate a crime. There is no great length of time in order to bring him under the law. An instant is as sufficient as a month to prove intent."

By ten-fifty-seven Mekota had completed his address. Judge Thompson at once began the reading of the instructions while the jurors paid the closest attention. They were a conscientious bunch and being on a jury for a murder trial was not something they had done before.

The court's instructions were as follows:

*First—the indictment in this case charges the defendant with the crime of murder.*

*For that he did on the 26th day of May, 1903, in Linn County, in the state of Iowa. With the specific intent to kill and murder, willfully, feloniously, deliberately and premeditatedly and of his malice aforethought shot one William Garrity then and there to-wit. May 26, 1903.*

*Second—to this charge the defendant has interposed a plea of not guilty. It is therefore incumbent upon the state to prove every fact essential to establish guilt, in order to warrant, conviction.*

*In order to do this the proof must be made fully. It must conform substantially to the allegations in the indictment, and must establish guilt beyond any reasonable doubt.*

*Third—a reasonable doubt is as the words import, a doubt of guilt which is founded in reason. It must be a real, substantial doubt, and not one that is merely fanciful or imaginary. It must not be sought after, nor should the evidence be strained to create or induce it. For when it is such a doubt as the law recognizes it must arise fairly and naturally in the mind upon a full consideration of all the facts and circumstances shown in evidence in the case.*

*If upon such consideration the mind hesitates and is unable to arrive at a conclusion of guilt that is entirely satisfactory to itself, this will be a reasonable doubt. And defendant should be given the benefit of it as such.*

*Fourth—if, however, the facts and circumstances proved are, in your judgment clear and satisfactory, as to exclude from your minds all such doubts, they should be taken as true. They go to the whole case and are against the defendant. You should convict of such offense as may be roved, as hereinafter stated.*

*Fifth—the facts essential in establishing guilt of the defendant. Or any such facts may be shown by evidence either direct or circumstantial.*

*Direct evidence is the evidence of witnesses to a fact or issue of which they have knowledge by means of their senses.*

*Circumstantial evidence is that which lends to establish a fact or facts in issue by the proof of collateral facts. From which it may be reasonably and logically deduced that the main or ultimate fact exists which is thus sought to be proved.*

*Sixth—in order, however, to warrant a conviction upon circumstantial evidence alone the facts proved must not only be consistent with the guilt of the accused, but they must also be inconsistent with any rational theory of his innocence.*

*Seventh—you are instructed that a rifle gun loaded with powder and ball is known and designated in law as a deadly weapon.*

*Eighth—the crime charged in the indictment is murder, but under the law it includes the following degrees of criminal homicide:*

*First; murder in the first degree; second; murder in the second degree, and third; manslaughter.*

*And if you find the defendant guilty you may convict him of either one of said degrees as you may find to be established beyond all reasonable doubt, as above instructed by the evidence under the rules of law as hereinafter given you.*

*And if there is in your minds a reasonable doubt of the degree of the crime of which the defendant is charged, you should convict the defendant only of the lower degree thereof of which you have no reasonable doubt, from all the evidence.*

*Ninth—murder in the first degree, as defined by law, is the willful, deliberate and premeditated killing of a human being with malice forethought.*

*The word willful as used in connection with the crime of murder means that the act is willed by the defendant. That it is purposely done with the intent to kill.*

*Deliberately means a well-considered purpose. Premeditatedly means with a fixed predetermined intention formed before the act. The lapse of time between the formation and the execution of such intention need not be long in point of time. It is sufficient if such intention is fully formed before the act.*

*Tenth—murder in the second degree is the unlawful killing of a human being with malice afore thoughts. Either expressed or implied, but without deliberation for premeditation.*

*Malice aforethought in the definition of murder does not necessarily mean hatred, spite or malevolence towards the deceased. But, instead, malice aforethought means that reckless disregard of the lives and safety of others which possessed those persons who intentionally and wantonly and wrongfully, with out just cause or excuse committed the act.*

*And is implied from every case of intentional homicide and inferred from the fact of the killing. It may also be inferred from the kind of weapon used, and the manner attending its use.*

*Eleventh—malice is essential to the crime of murder. It need not have existed for any considerable length of time. But it is sufficient if it existed for any length of time before the act of killing.*

*And if without such provinciality as is apparent sufficient to excite irritable passion, a person strike another with a deadly weapon likely to occasion death, although he had not previous malice, or ill-wish against the person struck, yet he is presumed in law to have had malice at the time that he inflicted the blow, and if death came from such blow, it will be murder in the first or second degree, depending on the facts or circumstances shown in evidence in the case.*

*Twelfth—manslaughter is the unlawful and felonious killing of one person by another without any malice expressed or implied, in a sudden quarrel, in a violent impulse of passion and upon reasonable provocation.*

*Thirteenth—if you find from the evidence beyond a reasonable doubt that at the time and place charged in the indictment herein, the defendant did willfully, deliberately, premeditatedly and with malice aforethought shoot the deceased, inflicting on his person a mortal wound from the effects of which the said deceased, William Garrity, then and there died, you should convict the defendant of murder in the first degree.*

*If you are not so satisfied from the said evidence, you should acquit the defendant of that degree.*

*If you find the defendant guilty of murder in the first degree, you will, as the law requires, designate in your verdict whether the defendant shall be punished by death or by imprisonment for life, at hard labor in the penitentiary.*

# Accountable: The Joseph Usher Story

*Fourteenth—it is claimed by defendant that at the time, or just prior to the time Garrity was shot, he, the defendant, had been assaulted by said Garrity, and whatever he did was in his own, proper self-defense against said assault.*

*Upon the law of this you are instructed, that the killing of an assailant is justifiable on the grounds of self-defense only when it reasonably appears to be the only answer.*

The Judge released the jury, who seemed somber and weary by eleven fifteen. The jurors filed directly to the jury room to deliberate their verdict. Joseph and his family watched them leave, one by one, and wondered what their decisions would be. Odd to think that people so separate from you can decide your fate. Intellectually the legal system made some sort of sense, but emotionally there could be no sanity found in its methodology.

The jury deliberated for nine long hours.

From Tuesday afternoon through evening Joseph and his relatives waited for their verdict. The time dragged. By eight in the evening, when it was apparent the jury would not soon agree, Judge Thompson announced he was going home and directed Joseph to do the same.

This was no great gift. Joseph could swallow no home cooking, nor could he find sleep beside his pregnant wife. He lay with his hands behind his head, starring at the ceiling and the upstairs of the house where William Garrity had been shot dead. Lucy fell asleep with her head pressed against Joseph's chest, and the sound of her soft breaths were the only comfort he could find in the darkness.

# Chapter 35

Joseph Usher and his family arrived in the city early on the morning of Wednesday, November 11, 1903. They traveled to Clarion on the eight o'clock train, and were in the courtroom before it had even begun to fill. Joseph was saddened that his daughter, Jennie, who had been devoted to her father, and had been by his side throughout the trial, could not be with him this last morning. Joseph's family had provided tremendous comfort during this drawn out ordeal—more than he ever could have imagined. As an adult male, working the land, and supporting his family, Joseph had not given much thought to needing the support of anyone else. He had felt self-sufficient. Of course he was teaching the boys to share his same strong work ethic, to perform their share of outdoor chores, and he had been able to rely on Lucy to keep up the household, but push come to shove, Joseph had the confidence to know he had it all under control until the night William Garrity was murdered.

On this day, Joseph sat silent at the end of the trial table. His two sons, Otto and George, were present, and they tried to will their strength to their father who appeared ashen and beyond fatigued. They noticed his downcast eyes, which only on occasion took a furtive sweep across the courtroom, and then lowered almost immediately as if he had made some sort of mistake in looking.

Joseph spoke to no one, not his brother nor his sons. Otto wondered if his father attempted to speak if he would be able to form any words. There is a strange thing that happens when a child crosses the threshold into adulthood, and has the opportunity to view his parent through a different lens. This happened on November 11, as Otto watched his father await his fate. For the first time, Otto saw his father as someone he needed to protect.

Attorneys Redmond and Smith were present, having arrived with Joseph just as the jury had finished eating breakfast. They filed back into the jury room, and Attorney Redmond knew intuitively that there would be no agreement reached before noon, no matter how much black coffee had been drunk. Attorney Smith stayed on with the Ushers while Attorney Redmond returned to Cedar Rapids; in addition, Attorneys Mekota and Crosby remained, waiting for news.

An hour passed, and then another. Finally, at 10:05, the bailiff, Mr. Grassfield, stepped out of the jury room and communicated with Judge Thompson who took the bench after their conversation. Attorney Smith spoke quietly to Joseph. With hesitation, Joseph stood and walked to a seat near the jury box. His nerves showed as his face twitched and his breathing quickened as if he were running–though he was practically still. There had been people loitering about in the corridors, as if they were waiting for something special, like a play or a concert to begin. Now they shuffled into the courtroom, but overall the courtroom was not filled as it had been on previous days. There was a stillness before the Judge even demanded it, until the tramping of the jury coming up the wooden staircase was heard. Bailiff Grassfield led the jury's procession, carrying the fatal rifle, and the blood-stained shirts. He carried the rest of the state's exhibits in a leather satchel. The jurors took their seats in the box and answered their names when called by Clerk Braska.

"Gentlemen of the jury," in the case of the state vs. Joseph Usher–charged with the murder of William Garrity–have you agreed upon your verdict?"

"We have," answered Foreman Reed. The verdict was passed to Judge Thompson who read:

"We, the jury, find the defendant guilty of manslaughter."

Joseph was motionless. He sat with his head down, as if in prayer, and his eyelids seemingly closed. He did not have the strength to meet the gaze of his sons. George, his eldest son, bowed his head into his outstretched hands. He squeezed his eyes shut when the word, "manslaughter" was spoken, as if he could shut out the verdict with this simple action. Otto wiped the tears from his eyes before his father looked up to see.

The jurors were then asked if that indeed was their verdict and each one replied in the affirmative. Judge Thompson then thanked them for the close attention they had given the case from beginning to end. "It is a source of great gratification for me. I am able to say to you at the close of this long trial. The trial has not at any time been delayed. Not for a single minute from waiting for any one of you." He informed them that they were discharged and, after reporting to the clerk's office, they were free to go home.

Attorney Smith stood and gave notice that a motion for a new trial would be filed. "I suppose that the defendant's bail will remain in force and that Mr. Usher will be released until the motion was heard and decided."

Judge Thompson replied, "Usher's bond is now inoperative. I remand Joseph to the custody of the sheriff." He made the following entry on the criminal calendar. *The jury returned the following verdict: We the jury, find the defendant guilty of manslaughter. Defendant remanded to the custody of the sheriff.* The Judge looked up and said, "The time for the adjournment of this term of court has arrived. The time for sentencing the defendant is fixed for Nov.12, 1903, at ten a.m." Attorney Smith had an exception noted, then the sheriff handcuffed Joseph.

He appeared docile and defeated. With his hands shackled together, Otto could not get a sense of who his father had been before all this had transpired. Joseph's son tried to force the present image of his cuffed father, standing before his eyes, to be replaced by the father he had preferred—the father who held leather reins in his hands, steering teams of strong horses, the father who could bend over and pick up a baby calf and sling it over his back. Now these images were hard to come by, and all Otto could sense was grief, a living grief, but nonetheless so strong it poured through him. He swallowed bravely as they took his father from the courtroom back to the jail he so loathed. Joseph would be held overnight, waiting for the sentence to be handed down the next day.

The next morning came as it always had, with the sun rising in the east, and the dampness from overnight drying as the light filtered down. The world did not reflect the woes of its people. Joseph witnessed this as he made his way back to the courtroom. When they came through the courtroom doorway, Joseph was disheartened to see every seat filled. Apparently there was great anticipation to see Joseph Usher sentenced. The one difference, every seat was taken by men. None of the women who had been attending all along were here on this final day. Perhaps due to their sympathy for the defendant, a man many of them had known well and trusted. Joseph Usher had not been the sort of neighbor who women found distasteful or avoided. In addition to his being respected by the community, the women may have felt too empathetic to see him sentenced to jail. It was not a far stretch of the imagination to think these women would have no trouble picturing themselves in such a tragic predicament, and Lucy's pregnancy only further elicited sympathy from the female population in Linn County. Not one woman in that region would think she, herself, could handle what poor Lucy Usher was going through. Better their husbands attend the sentencing and tell them about it over a hot supper, in the comfort of their homes, then watch the awful conclusion play out right in front of them.

Sheriff Evans ushered Joseph to his seat at the table. Isaac, Joseph's brother, and Otto and George, were in the chairs directly next to him. They could sense the nervous energy coming from Joseph like static electricity.

Judge Thompson spoke. "Gentleman, in the case of the state against Joseph Usher, the hour fixed for the sentence has arrived."

# Chapter 36

Attorney Clemens arose and read the following motion to set aside the verdict and to grant the defendant a new trial:

*Thursday November 12, 1903*

*Motion for a New Trial:*

*In the Iowa District court within and for Linn County, September term, 1903.*

*The State of Iowa vs. Joseph Usher, defendant*

*No. 2387 Motion for new trial.*

*Comes now the defendant herein, Joseph Usher, and moves the court to set aside the verdict of the jury rendered on the 11th day of November, 1903, in the above entitled cause, finding him guilty of manslaughter, and asks for a new trial in said case upon the following grounds:*

*(1) The court erred in admitting evidence offered and introduced by the state over the defendant's objections, to which rulings of the court the defendant excepted at the time, which evidence, the objection thereto, the rulings of the court thereon and exceptions taken thereto, are all*

*preserved and shown in the official reporter's shorthand notes of the trial.*

*(2) The court erred in excluding certain evidence and testimony offered by the defendant, on objections made by the state, to which rulings of the court exception were taken by the defendant at the time; which evidence, objections by the state, the rulings of the court thereon and exception taken thereto by the defendant, all appear in the record and minutes of the official shorthand reporter's notes of the trial.*

*(3) The court erred in giving to the jury the 1st, 2nd, 3rd, 4th, 5th, 6th, 7th 8th, 9th, 10th, 11th, 12, 13th, 14th, 15th, 16th, 17th, 18th, 19th, and 20th instruction of the court's charge to the jury, to each and every one of which instructions, and as an entirety, exceptions were taken by the defendant at the time and entered into the record by the official shorthand reporter.*

*(4) The court erred in stating in writing at the bottom thereof, that the 5th instruction was asked by the defendant, as it was not asked by the defendant, but given on the court's own motion in lieu of the 4th and 5th instructions asked by the defendant.*

*(5) The court erred in refusing to give the 1st, 2d, 3d, 4th, 5th, 6th, 7th and 8th instructions asked by the defendant, all of which said instructions so asked and refused appear of record in the case in the office of the clerk of the district court of said county.*

*(6) There was misconduct of counsel on behalf of the state made during the progress of the trial in remarks, exclamations and declarations made in the presence of the jury about the defendant himself during the progress of the trial, by uttering insinuating remarks and ridiculing the witnesses of the*

defense, all of which is shown by the official shorthand reporter's notes of the trial of the case; that such remarks and misconduct of counsel on the part of the state were persisted in over objections made thereto by defendant's counsel and the court erred in many of the instances in not admonishing counsel to abstain from such misconduct.

(7) There was manifest error on the part of the court in making remarks derogatory to the defendant's witnesses during the progress of the trial, and observations of the impact and effect of the evidence during the progress of the trial.

There was a mulish error in the progress of the trial also in this: That counsel for the state in the opening argument to the jury, after the conclusion of the testimony, distorted and misrepresented the evidence to the jury and asserted on his own personal knowledge that he had ideas about the motive for the crime, and in gesticulations. In pointing out the defendant and calling him harsh and blasphemous names, among which were: the defendant was a damnable cur and habitual criminal.

(8) The court erred in refusing to send into the jury room and by the bailiff to the jury, by request of defendant's counsel, exhibits "H" and "I" introduced in evidence by the state, the first being the statement written down by witness Lazell in longhand and signed by the defendant: Usher, as claimed by the state: the second being the longhand transcript of the shorthand minutes of an alleged statement of the defendant, taken by the witness W. E. Holmes.

(9) The court erred in refusing to send with the bailiff and into the jury room for the consideration of the jury on its retirement the said exhibits referred to in the eight error herein above assigned at the request of counsel for the state.

*(10) The court erred in permitting over the defendant's objections, the attorney for the state to cross examine its own witness, Otto Usher, when the record shows that he was neither an unwilling witness nor one that evaded a question or prevaricated in any of his answers, nor manifested any hostility to the prosecution or undue bias in favor of the defendant.*

*(11) The verdict is not sustained by the evidence.*

*(12) The verdict is the result of passion and prejudice of the jury, and not of a fair, candid deliberation on its part.*

*(13) The court erred in refusing to receive in evidence exhibits "H" and "I" offered by the state, unless the defendant agreed thereto.*

*(14) The court by his constant urging counsel to hurry in the introduction of their evidence prevented counsel for the defendant from exercising the care and prudence requisite to a safe conduct of the defense to the charge of the crime of that contained in the indictment.*

*(15) The court erred in failing to instruct the jury that they might find the defendant guilty of an assault, and the court was guilty of misconduct in refusing to so instruct the jury when the jury so requested him after their retirement to consider their verdict, as shown by the accompanying affidavit.*

*(16) His failing to give the jury an instruction defining assault.*

*(17) In overruling defendant's motion for a continuance and forcing him to trial while ill.*

Attorney Clemens finished reading the motion for a new trial and looked at Judge Thompson who immediately asked, "Have you anything further to say on your motion Mr. Clemens?"

"Nothing, your honor."

Judge Thompson promptly overruled the motion for a new trial, and Joseph Usher realized how you could be so wrong in believing things could not possibly get any worse. The Judge directed Joseph to approach the bench and receive his dreaded sentence. Joseph Usher rose. He paused after he stood. The new brown suit Attorney Redmond had purchased for him when the trial began, was already hanging loosely on his thin frame. Joseph walked to the Judge's desk, and Otto thought his father almost resembled a boy in trouble with the head schoolmaster. He seemed nervous, as if he were going to have to hold out his hand for a slapping with a ruler.

"You have been indicted for the crime of murder in the first degree," the Judge declared. "You have been tried and the jury has found you guilty of manslaughter. The time for the final disposition of this matter and the passing of sentence has now arrived. Have you anything to say why sentence should not be passed upon you?"

Joseph replied in a low tone. "All I have to say is that I am an innocent man."

A sigh was emitted by the crowd. Joseph's family could not tell if it was a sigh of relief or disbelief.

Judge Thompson then asked Redmond, "Do you have anything to say for the defendant?"

Mr. Redmond replied, "I have nothing particularly to say, Your Honor. You heard the trial and you know how the jury stood, and how this matter was considered by them. I am informed by one of the jurymen that there were five for acquittal in the beginning of their conference. And that after being in consultation for hours this verdict was returned as the best that they could agree upon. The best that could be done and it was brought in. It's apparent that this man is guilty of willful murder or he is innocent.

He is a man that is past the median of life. He has been a good citizen and a hard worker. He is a man of a family and a grandfather.He has always been peaceable and we think that the verdict is unjust. But probably the best judgment the jury had or could exercise on the case under all the circumstances. We ask your honor to be lenient and to take into consideration the possibility that this man is wholly innocent."

Joseph Usher stood stone still, his breathing exaggerated beneath his suit jacket. Otto recognized his father's fear; he had seen this fear in the animals he had hunted in the woods—when he had come upon a deer or a rabbit he was aiming to shoot with his rifle.

Judge Thompson spoke once more. "Joseph A. Usher you having been found guilty of manslaughter by the petit jury, you are hereby sentenced to five years at hard labor in the state penitentiary at Anamosa. You are to pay the costs of the prosecution."

With a large bang of his mallet Judge Thompson then declared the court to be adjourned.

Josephs Usher's attorneys immediately gave notice of an appeal to the supreme court of Iowa. In addition they filed an appeal bond in the sum of five thousand dollars–signed by four of Joseph's relatives, and approved by Clerk Braska.

At this point Joseph Usher was released. He and his family caught the eleven a.m. car back to Cedar Rapids where they retrieved their horses and buggy and drove directly home. Exhaustion had long ago settled in and all they wanted was a warm bed to crawl into where they could shut out the events of the day. Joseph took off his brown trial suit and hoped he would never have to feel the wool fabric against his skin again. The suit had become a reminder of a time he'd rather forget. He would happily put on his farm clothes in the morning and not touch his shaver. He crawled into bed next to Lucy and felt the warmth of his frightened wife and his unborn child. If he could shut out the world and stay cocooned here for the rest of his days, he would do so with no complaints.

# Chapter 37

On the morning of Friday, November 13, 1903, Smith filed the following statement for the defendant. This statement was notarized by John M. Redmond, the Notary Public of Linn County, Iowa.

*I, M.P. Smith being duly sworn, depose and say that I was one of the attorneys for the defendant in the trial of the case of the state of Iowa vs. Joseph Usher, at the present term of court.*

*That on the morning of the 12th day of November, 1903, and while the jury were yet considering their verdict, about at nine-thirty a.m. of said day the bailiff brought into the court room and delivered a verbal communication to the judge from the jury.*

*That the judge, the Hon. Wm. G. Thompson, at once informed me the jury had requested to know whether or not they could return, or would be permitted to return, a verdict against the defendant finding him guilty of an assault, and that he (the said judge) had instructed the bailiff that he should inform the jury that he would give them no further instructions than what he had, and that they should find the* defendant guilty of one of the degrees of homicide described in the instructions, or not guilty; and that the said bailiff, to-wit, Peter Grassfield, at once retired to the jury room and afterward informed me that he delivered the court's message directly to the jury.

(Signed.) M.P. Smith

Subscribed and sworn to by M.P. Smith, this 13th day of November, 1903.

John M. Redmond, Notary Public in and for Linn County, Iowa.

Attorney Redmond sent a message to Joseph that his appeal to the Iowa Supreme Court had been filed and the pending decision of the Court would not be expected in less than eighteen month's time. Attorney Redmond also claimed the counsel for the defense was sanguine that the Supreme Court would grant him a new trial. Joseph Usher was additionally informed that the counsel for the state was equally sanguine that the verdict of the trial court would be sustained.

Joseph was relieved to receive this message, even though it was a mixed one. He now knew that he was guaranteed a year and a half to be with his family and try to regain the momentum and normalcy of his day-to- day life. In a case like this, denial doesn't count for much, but it could be counted on to go a little way, like a small bandage, and for now that was good enough.

Lucy was elated that Joseph was home at least for now. She could worry about a new trial later. On Saturday, November 14, Lucy knew instinctively that her baby was to be born. She was overcome with a nervous energy and yet, she understood without being told, that she should get some rest. Saturday afternoon wore on, and Lucy sat with her feet up, letting Otto, Walter and Joseph do all the household chores. Joseph would take a break between working and come give his wife's hand a squeeze. They were never so glad to have quiet time at home, and being the sort who found something to be grateful even in the most trying situations, the Ushers were entirely thankful that the trial had ended in time for Joseph to be home with his wife when she went into labor.

After the supper chores were finished, Lucy noticed the first of her labor pains beginning in her lower back. The night was going to be a long one, and Joseph could see how frightened and excited his wife was. Fortunately for Lucy, she was not ignorant when it came to childbirth. She had watched and helped her mother with her births, so she certainly knew what to expect, even if she didn't know exactly how it would feel.

Early in the morning the midwife came. She was an older woman from their neighborhood, and the presence of another female immediately put Lucy at ease.

Joseph sent Otto to fetch Dr. Lockwood, as well, since Lucy's condition was delicate. This was to be a Sunday child: "And the child that is born on the Sabbath day is bonny and blithe, and good and gay." This thought made Lucy content.

When Dr. Lockwood arrived, shortly after noon, Lucy and the midwife were doing quite well, but she still was happy that Joseph had sent for him to come. Not long after he scrubbed up and came to Lucy's side, she was ready to give the last hard push. Dr. Lockwood caught the beautiful baby girl as she came into this world, while her mother cried and smiled at the same time.

Lucy had never felt such sheer exhaustion, and when the baby wailed she was flooded with relief and joy. Lucy knew all the things that could go wrong with a birthing, but she and her baby daughter had been most fortunate.

Otto and Walter returned to the farmhouse just in time to see their father presented with his new baby daughter. This was the first time the boys had seen their father beam without the slightest bit of sadness since the tragic death of William Garrity.

Dr. Lockwood handed the tiny bundle to Joseph, and in his arms his baby girl looked even tinier. The brothers thought their baby sister was the cutest baby they had ever seen. They had decided to name her Linnie Isabel Usher. Now Walter could be a big brother too, and this made him immeasurably proud. Walter held his baby sister's hand in his own with a look of disbelief on his face. Joseph laughed when looking at his youngest son, thinking his chest was as puffed up as a proud father's.

The night of Linnie's birth, the boys kept the stove fired up for their baby sister and for Lucy. The nights had turned cold and the days were cool. From outside the farmhouse, Joseph could smell the wood stove burning, and he breathed in deeply, thinking there was nothing better in the world than a warm, well-lit house and your family inside. As the days passed, he watched with relief and pride as Lucy settled into being a new mother. The worry of a new trial seemed far away. The Ushers' focus was baby Linnie, and how she thrived as winter set in all around them.

# Chapter 38

**March 2, 1904. Joseph A. Usher to George D. O'Connell, Warranty deed. nw. nw. 27 83-8 $3,250.**

On Wednesday, December 14, 1904, Major Milo P. Smith and Honorable John M. Redmond, counsel for Joseph Usher appeared in Des Moines, Iowa, before the Supreme Court to submit the appeal for their client, presenting both written and oral arguments. The Supreme Court stated that a decision would be handed down within the next two or three months. Both attorneys felt confident about their appeal for Joseph, and certain there was a very strong chance for a new trial.

On Tuesday, January 10, 1905, the Supreme Court reversed the judgment of the trial court in the case of Joseph Usher, who had been convicted at the November 1903 term of district court for manslaughter, having been charged with the murder of William Garrity, a hired man. Joseph's council had put up an appeal bond, going to the Supreme Court on error in the trial, which remanded the case for a new trial.

The conviction of Joseph Usher was reversed because Judge Thompson, before whom the trial was held, did not instruct the jury that, since the defendant's plea was self-defense, it was necessary for the state to prove–beyond a reasonable doubt–that he was not acting in self-defense. This is an important matter for defendants in such prosecutions, and was discussed at some length by Justice Sherwin.

Justice Sherwin said, in part, that the instruction of Judge Thompson on this point was calculated to impress on the jury that it was up to the defendants to establish Joseph Usher's defense, and, failing therein, he should be convicted. The instruction was as follows:

"If you find from the evidence that the defendant, at the time and place in question, was assaulted by the said William Garrity, and that from the nature and character of the assault upon him. It reasonably appeared to him, as a reasonably prudent, courageous and cautious man, that he was about to suffer death or great bodily harm to himself by reason of the said assault, and that it further so appeared to him that the gun in question was the only means of saving his life or preventing great bodily harm to himself, then he would be justified in using the gun. But no instruction to the effect that the burden was on the state to show that the defendant was not acting in self-defense was given, although one was asked."

"It should have been given," said the court.

"The defendant admitted the killing, and justified it on the ground of self-defense. It was therefore of the greatest importance to him that the jury be told that it must be satisfied beyond a reasonable doubt that he was not acting in self-defense when he killed Garrity. There was a failure in this respect, and the instruction that was given may easily have been understood as placing the burden on the defendant.

Absolutely nothing was brought out in the trial to show a motive on Joseph's part for the shooting.

On the other hand, the defense established the fact that Garrity was a dissipated man. That he had been on a prolonged drinking bout just previous to his death, and that his actions had been peculiar on the day of the tragedy.

The state urged two pieces of alleged circumstantial evidence in the prosecution of the case. One was that the Usher family burned all the bedding and the bed on which Garrity was found by the neighbors who had been summoned. The other was that the weapon with which the killing was done was found hidden in an oats bin. Aside from these, the statements of the Ushers were very much mixed and in a measure contradictory."

# Chapter 39

On Wednesday, January 11, 1905, Joseph Usher received the long-awaited word from Attorney Smith and Redmond that he was to have a new trial. Linnie was just over two years old, and spent her days toddling about after her family. The Ushers were elated; they prayed this new trial contained at least a glimmer of hope, since the wait had been long and had affected their nerves. Lucy especially. Joseph watched day by day as his wife's nerves wore thin. He could tell by the furrow on her brow and the hard line her mouth took as she did her chores. Linnie brought out the smile in her mother, but the light left Lucy's face in an instant, and Joseph could see how easily she returned to her worrisome thoughts.

Perhaps it was the not knowing that was the hardest. The Ushers could not plan on their future since they had no way of discerning what their future held. Otto was proud of his father's strength, and thought he handled the stress of waiting for a new trial with steely determination. What concerned Joseph most, Otto knew, was his concern for Lucy.

He could not let himself think what would happen to their family if he was sent away to prison and Lucy were left to fend for them without his support.

Lucy insisted she would attend the second trial no matter its outcome. Monday, May 14, 1906 arrived as spring had taken root on the Usher's farm. Linnie and Walter spent time outdoors, the two year old chasing after her big brother, and for the fist time really taking notice of everything in the outside world around her—the blades of grass moving in the wind, a robin flying over head, or the yellow crocuses poking out from the dark soil. Linnie's enthusiasm was contagious, and just what the Usher's needed for distraction. There was no better sound than her laughter—which was not clouded by any of the troubles her parents and brothers carried.

Once again, the neighbors rallied around and gave their support. The Spicer's kindly offered for Linnie and Walter to stay with them during the trial. The children, thank goodness, were oblivious to the seriousness of the second trial, and that's the way Joseph and Lucy wanted it to be. There was no need for their children to be robbed of their innocence.

The Usher family once again gathered at the district court, showing strong support for Joseph, being tried for the second time for the murder of William Garrity. The courtroom was crowded every day, with as high an interest in this trial as there had been in the first—it seemed as though no one had forgotten the case and if anything curiosity had only grown stronger in two year's time. This time Judge Preston presided over the proceedings in this bitterly contested case. Nearly all the testimony presented at this trial was taken from the written transcript of the first case.

The afternoon of May 17, once both sides had presented their cases with diligence, Judge Preston sent the jury out to deliberate with his careful instructions.

The tension and anticipation were present in the courtroom. Lucy could hardly bear the stress, and her body betrayed her emotion by trembling as she sat with the Usher family. She remembered all too well the previous trial, and carrying Linnie in her stomach as she sat worrying about her husband's fate. Now she felt alone and frightened. Lucy could not contemplate weeks, months, or years without Joseph by her side. She tried to imagine where she would find the strength and came up empty handed.

There were so many folks Lucy knew who were worse off, she tried to remind herself of this, and how they carried on with dignity and grace, but Lucy recognized she was cut from different cloth, weaker cloth, and there was little she could do to muster the strength she needed. Lucy watched Joseph, whom she believed had somehow made himself numb to the proceedings in the courtroom. He sat stone still, his breathing shallow, and his face void of emotion. Joseph was her life; he was her one love.

The bailiff came into the courtroom andwalked directly to the judge, whispering, "The jury has decided their verdict."

Judge Preston brought his mallet down and called everyone back to be seated. Once again the steady trampling of the juror's feet sounded as they climbed the wooden stairs. Lucy felt such dread in her heart as they entered the courtroom and took their places. Otto moved to the front of his chair. The time was four thirty, and the jurors had taken only two and a half hours to deliberate. Otto glanced at Lucy, but she did not meet his gaze, nor did his father. The bailiff handed Judge Preston the hand-written verdict:

*We, the jury, find the defendant guilty of manslaughter in the murder of William Garrity.*

Joseph heard the verdict but bore no emotion. He took a deep breath as if he may not be able to take another, and listened as Judge Preston continued with his sentence. He called Joseph up to the stand. Lucy held her hands to her face, as if she could hide from the public.

The Judge was speaking, but all Joseph Usher could discern was, "I sentence you to eight years of hard labor in the penitentiary at Anamosa." With this announcement, Lucy stood, and rushed to the attorney's table. She let out a blood-curdling scream as she pounded on the table, "No! No! No!"

Joseph was handcuffed and taken into custody as his inconsolable wife was restrained by the officers. Otto watched as both his parents were led away. He thought immediately of Walter and Linnie, and what he would say to comfort his poor younger siblings. He had no idea.

Attorney Redmond once again filed an appeal to the Iowa Supreme Court. This was no comfort to the Ushers.

Lucy was taken to the police station, and then transferred immediately to the Cedar Rapids' Hospital. After an evaluation, it was determined that Lucy was in a shattered state, and therefore needed to be admitted to a hospital for the insane.

Meanwhile, Joseph was bonded out of jail until further notice from the Iowa Supreme Court. He went straight to his wife's side, and found her burdened with uncontrollable grief. Joseph had never seen her that dark, even though he had witnessed her outbreaks worsening over the past couple of years. He could think of nothing to console her. Lying was pointless, and only his not having to serve a sentence would bring Lucy the relief she needed to climb out of her despair.

Joseph tried to remember the sweet young woman he had first met at the Reverend's house, and how free of troubles she had been. If he thought far enough back he could recall the sound of her laughter, and how it made his heart light.

Joseph agreed with the doctors that Lucy should be taken to the Independence mental hospital. Hopefully the treatment she would receive would result in a healthy recovery, and the restoration of her faculties. After all, she had recovered the last time. Joseph felt guilt over Lucy's condition; he couldn't help but conjecture that if she had married differently, perhaps her mental health never would have suffered. Of course, at the back of his mind, too, was his affair with Hulda, and how this indiscretion had scarred his poor wife. There were things he would do differently if he were given a chance.

Joseph and Otto, father and son, shared similar worries—ones that concerned Linnie and Walter, Lucy's mental health, the insurmountable attorney fees, as well as the future of their farm. These were all enormous concerns, but at least they carried them together as one day gave way to another.

# Chapter 40

On Tuesday, May 7, 1907, Joseph received the news from Attorney Redmond that he would be sent to the penitentiary for eight years unless he received a pardon. The Supreme Court affirmed the sentence mandated by Judge Preston. Joseph and his family cried upon receiving this dire news. This was the axe that had been poised above their heads since the night William Garrity was murdered.

Attorney Redmond watched the Ushers gather together with their heads down and their spirits all but gone. He swallowed hard and turned away, looking out of the farmhouse windows to the tall grasses and the trees on the Usher's land. Hard to believe such a peaceful place could be so riddled with discord and strife.

Redmond and his team had worked long and hard to defend Joseph Usher. He felt the need to tell his client, in person, the news handed down by the Supreme Court. Joseph, as well as his family, had earned a great deal of respect from the Attorney and the rest of the team. Redmond felt it was generally believed by those who had studied this complicated case—most particularly himself—that the story of the killing of William Garrity's death had never really been told. Furthermore, in his heart, he knew if the actual events of that tragic night could be fully recounted, Joseph Usher would be proven an innocent man, but at this point in time, the verdict and the sentence were regarded as irrefutable and correctly handed down.

Attorney Redmond stayed with the Ushers and visited instead of rushing back to town. He had grown fond of this family and genuinely cared how they were faring without Lucy in the household, and with Joseph soon to be gone. Linnie had grown since the last time he visited. She was three and a half and running about like a miniature Lucy, without any troubles to cloud her cherubic little face.

Joseph and his attorney watched Linnie playing as her father spoke about how the child had missed her mother greatly. Fortunately, Joseph's stepmother, Mrs. Steadman, had been helping out considerably, and the little girl had come to love her, and look to her for comfort and love. Grandmother Steadman was genuinely kind to the family.

Joseph was grateful for this love and support. He never imagined Lucy would be ill for so long. But thank goodness there was still love in the house, and with Grandmother Steadman there was also the much-needed influence of a woman. Redmond commented how tall Walter had grown, and this made the boy beam. Walter longed for the day he would stand eye to eye with his big brother, Otto, and although it would be quite some time, he still enjoyed entertaining the thought. Otto had grown taller and more handsome, filling out as a young man does without even noticing.

He stood proud, on this sad day, despite the bad news the Ushers had been given.

After some conversation, Redmond said goodbye to the Ushers and told Joseph that he would be notified when to appear at the prison. He would be given a little time to prepare. Joseph's only wish was that he, himself, would arrive to the prison, without a humiliating police escort. The Judge let it be known that this sort of protocol was not typical, but in this case he would make an exception. Attorney Smith traveled down to Anamosa and informed the warden, Mr. Marguis Barr, that he would be personally responsible for Joseph's behavior. As Attorney Redmond rode away from the Usher's farm, with Linnie running circles in the sun, and Walter and Otto watching after their little sister like protective brothers, he thought how much he wished this poor family could have been left intact.

# Chapter 41

Wednesday, January 8th, 1908, arrived all too soon. Joseph had received official word that he was to go to the State Reformatory at Anamosa. Grandma Steadman had come out to the farm and was all set to keep house for Walter and Otto while their father was away. Joseph could not believe he had reached this point of acceptance, but he had; he was ready to go into servitude. This is how a man goes from being who he was, an independent and honorable member of society, successfully running a dairy farm, supporting his wife and children, respected by all who knew him, to a man stripped of everything he had worked for, a man reduced to nothing but his own flesh and blood and prison garb, serving time that is not his own. The hardest thing for Joseph Usher was having to walk away from his boys and Linnie. This would be the thing that would cause him to sit up in bed, startled from a deep sleep, and imagine his family struggling along without him.

Lucy's family from nearby Centerville had requested caring for Linnie. Joseph agreed this would be for the best.

Linnie was now five years old and had many needs. His daughter required female guidance and Joseph knew that Lucy's family would provide her with all the love and learning necessary to become a worthwhile young girl. He worried about Linnie who would now feel the loss of another parent along with her two loving brothers. These thoughts gave Joseph a large lump in his throat. If he could change the events of this tragic misfortune for any reason, it would be for Linnie and Lucy—the two he felt suffered the most from the tragic death of William Garrity. Joseph was aware that Walter and Otto were hearty and had one another to cling to—at least there was that comfort.

Joseph requested of Otto that he go with him to Anamosa and then bring back his civilian clothes. Father and son drove to town early in the morning. The winter sun was dim in the whitened sky as they made their way, and the cold traveled right down to Joseph's bones. They turned their horse into the feed stable and boarded the train for Anamosa at nine o'clock in the morning. Joseph suggested they get a cup of coffee and a slice of pie, as this may be the last good meal he would taste for quite some time. Otto preferred to think his father would not suffer so with bad food or meager accommodations. He was impressed how his father resigned himself to the events that had befallen them—first the awful trials, then Lucy's mental collapse, as well as having to provide for a family with no wife and mother, and now, of course, his prison sentence. Otto could not imagine having such strength himself. He hoped he had inherited some of his father's steely ability to cope.

After lunch, which Joseph ate slowly, savoring his coffee

and every morsel of food, they walked quietly down the street to the penitentiary and requested the warden. Otto thought how odd this was. His father requesting the warden could just as well been a request for some feed for their cattle. Joseph spoke calmly and with little emotion. The officer at the door informed the Ushers that the warden was far too busy to see visitors at that hour of the day, but Otto explained their peculiar situation and the officer decided to escort them to the front office. The warden soon met Joseph and his son and explained it would be necessary for certain routines to be followed. Otto wanted to know if he could see his father once more before returning home. Otto was informed that he could return in a couple of hours, which he did, meeting his father for the first time in regulation clothes. They visited for a time before the guard came in, and told the young man he could return later in the day to pick up Joseph's civilian clothes. When Otto fetched his father's clothing, the prison authorities told him Joseph had gone out to the farm located approximately three-fourth's mile up the railroad track to Cedar Rapids. Late that afternoon Otto rode the train back home to the farm. He peered out the window at the farm buildings and he could just make out his father, standing in the farm yard, waving his hand as the train traveled by slowly. Tears came to Otto's eyes and he bit his lip when he laid eyes on his father. As sad as it was to see his father in this new place, in unfamiliar clothes, he had a strong sense that he would be fine; Joseph Usher would make it through this sentence.

Grandma Steadman was waiting for Otto when he returned home. She was greatly relieved to hear how things had turned out. She, too, had to remain positive. Joseph could handle this sentence, and his family would be fine in his absence. Otto let Grandma Steadman know that he was permitted to visit his father in one week's time, and then his visits would be permitted once monthly. There was a comfort in knowing he and his father would see each other with regularity. Otto was coming to learn that even during times of duress there were small comforts to be had.

When Wednesday morning, January 15, arrived, Otto awoke for the first time with joy, knowing he was to see his father whom he missed more than he thought possible. He worried about what frame of mind his father would be in after the first week of his sentence, and as he worried he also offered Walter comfort since he was bemoaning the fact he, too, could not go visit. Walter complained to Otto that he never got to go anywhere. Otto knew his little brother's frustrations, but could do nothing to change the rules and regulations of the jail. He promised Walter that he would tell him every bit of his conversation with their father, and that he would be sure to give his father Walter's love.

Otto found his father looking well. They stood back and took one another in as if more than seven days had gone by, then they shook hands and hugged. Joseph told his son all about his routine.

The first day, shortly after dinner, a farm manager came for Joseph, and explained exactly what was expected of him. Otto wanted to have a picture in his head of how his father lived and what he did day-to-day. Joseph explained that there was a hog house with an alley through the middle, with an office at the end, next to the foreman's house.

Joseph had a coffee pot on a stove in the room, and a cot for sleeping. Joseph's job was to watch the brood sows, or feeding hogs, and make sure they were well tended and the pens were kept clean. There were young men on hand to help with any heavy work that needed to be done.

On the first night, at five a.m., a guard came to his door and called him for breakfast. The cook was preparing a meal in the kitchen for all the inmates. The guard introduced Joseph to the cook who was also an inmate. Once the guard had left, the old cook explained to Joseph that they would be eating their breakfast together, and if there were anything good to eat in the house, he would be sure to see that they got their share. After the men had eaten breakfast, Joseph was handed a lit lantern and directed to find his way out to the farm, which he had already been shown the day before.

Otto felt a sense of relief as his father spoke of the farm and his duties. Joseph's son knew that having the opportunity to work the farm was an outlet and a blessing for a man who could not have understood or adjusted to being confined indoors. At least not without a toll being taken over time.

Joseph went on to describe the man who supervised the farm—a civilian—not an inmate. He and his wife and family lived in a decent home situated near the buildings. He told Otto that the farm was familiar and the food was as good as anyone could wish. The meat was raised and fattened on the farm, and they lacked nothing; there was even plenty of good cream, the bread was baked right in the kitchen, the butter was sweet and produced from the farm's herd. He and the cook were content with the lot they had been dealt.

A look of relief passed between father and son. Otto knew

from listening to his father that he was going to get along as well anyone could in these circumstances, and for this he was grateful. Otto was anxious to return to the Usher's farm and tell Grandma Steadman and Walter his good news. If only Lucy was as fortunate in her situation. Her recovery would have meant the world to Joseph.

# Chapter 42

Linnie had settled in with her mother's family, and although she missed her home, her father, and her two big brothers, she had adapted well, and this had made her family feel comforted by their unwanted separation. Linnie was growing, and looking more and more like her mother. If Lucy could have laid her eyes on her sweet little daughter, or held her in her arms, she may have found the strength to pull herself from the abyss she had fallen into, but everyone knew it wasn't a conscious choice for Lucy to be ill, nor anything over which she had the least bit of control.

Later in the year of 1908, Lucy's family complained about having the responsibility of raising Linnie. Perhaps when they took on the task, they did not realize just how long their responsibility for Linnie would be, and there was an expense that accompanied raising a child whom they could no longer afford.

This situation greatly upset Joseph, who had little or no control of things outside the prison's walls. Joseph talked to Otto about Linnie's circumstances. He explained he had discussed Linnie with the farm manager at the prison, who then conferred with his wife. As good fortune would have it, they decided Linnie could be brought to live at their home, and Joseph could see his daughter each and every day.

Otto discussed the matter with Attorney Redmond, and was then directed to travel down to Centerville where he was to talk to Lucy's family. Otto was happy to see his little sister, and she evidently was thrilled to see him. She leapt into his arms and wrapped herself around her big, strong brother, seeming like she never intended on letting go. Lucy's family heard Otto's solution to his sister's dilemma, and after careful consideration they decided to keep Linnie with them; everyone agreed this was for the best, although deep inside Joseph was sorrowful that he would not see his Linnie with any regularity. He was grateful that the farm manager and his wife were willing to accommodate his child and help in such a trying situation—though their kindness was never called upon.

Otto and Joseph were faced with other dilemmas as well. The two discussed these matters during their monthly visits. They knew, all too well, that they would have to sell their home soon. The expenses for the trials and litigation were needing to be paid, and there were other expenses involved as well, that kept Joseph awake much of the night. If it were not for these monumental expenses, Otto felt certain that he and Grandma Steadman, along with Walter, could have managed quite well.

Otto thought long and hard about his father's life and how it turned. At first, it seemed, his father led a charmed life, almost like a fairy tale. He worked hard, paid his debts, never had any trouble whatsoever with the law, and he was well-liked in a community he had set up roots in and then remained. Otto, nor anyone else, could not fathom why his father would have shot William Garrity in cold-blooded murder or otherwise. No matter how hard Otto examined the events, he could not make sense of its tragic parts.

# Chapter 43

*S*aturday, September 19, 1908, representatives of The *Gazette visited the Reformatory at Anamosa and interviewed Warden Barr and Deputy Smith. During this interview, the journalists were informed by the Warden and Deputy that managing a "colony" of older offenders was far easier than handling three or four hundred young men. The older veterans had the presence of mind to know they must obey every rule of the institution in to enjoy the privileges available. The younger prisoners had much to learn in this regard. In addition, the reporters were informed that the natural inclination of the young prisoners was to talk, and the talkers had the most trouble and the greatest number of infractions of discipline.*

There was a large book in Deputy Warder Smith's office, in which all the complaints were entered. Every day there were complaints filed, and surprisingly, the majority of these entries were for violation of rules against talking. The difficulty of not being permitted to speak when sitting down to meals, or attending chapel, or working—for that matter—not having *the privilege of uttering something of value to your nearest neighbor, was a prison unto itself. As the reporters from the newspaper spoke to the Warden and Deputy, the men knew intrinsically how vital communication and freedom of expression were to daily life. The act of conversing was often the single biggest aspect of a man's life to help keep him sane and functioning.*

*The warden let the journalists know that more modern methods of prison management were being adopted. Efforts were also being made to improve the sanitary conditions, to make the prison more humane. However, they were still wrestling with the question of whether or not the young criminals should or could be housed together in the same institution as the older and more experienced criminals. There were a great deal of questions and speculation regarding prison management that needed to be investigated and given careful thought. This was certain.*

*After the journalists were done speaking with the Warden and Deputy, they went on to have private chats with several of the prisoners, including Joseph Usher, Frank S. Smith and I.R. Van Tassel. Speaking to the men, themselves, was good insight into prison life, and gave a different perspective than the one they had already gained from talking to the prison officials.*

*As far as Joseph Usher's interview, the newspaper reporter found he was a "trusty," who worked with a small gang on the state farm. He made note that Joseph Usher came and went as he worked day in and day out, all without a guard or a watch of any kind.*

*Naturally, Mr. Usher is hopeful that he will be paroled before long and hopes he will eventually be pardoned. He undoubtedly will be paroled.*

*Those who are familiar with later developments in his case confidently believe him to be an innocent man, and that he is suffering for the mistake of another, whom he would shield. Perhaps Mr. Usher made a mistake in not telling the whole story at the time of his arrest. While one cannot but admire him for his courage, one cannot help but wonder if any rule of honor requires such unselfish sacrifice. But Joseph Usher will return unimpaired with all his mental faculties alert and his conscience clear.*

# Chapter 44

The last winter Otto and Walter had with their Grandma in the old home was bittersweet. Otto enjoyed his Grandmother's company, since they were short on family, and she was a pleasant and loving woman. They took her to visit some of her old friends around Covington: Mrs. Ribble, and Mr. and Mrs. Dickenson, who lived near the old Perry Usher place. Grandma also loved to visit Mrs. Burt, who lived by the railroad bridge just east of Covington. All these visits were a welcome distraction for the Ushers; other people's company, the music of laughter and light-hearted conversation, all provided normalcy and much-needed companionship. Grandma was a magnet for social visits. In the evening, Floyd Weed and his younger sisters, Ina and Miley, could come visit, playing caroms while eating a delicious lunch, of course served by Grandma, who knew how to be a wonderful hostess. Otto loved to see his Grandma's face flushing with laughter, and her eyes dancing with joy as she talked to her guests.

They knew when the early spring of 1909 arrived, the Usher's home had to be vacated since George Stark, their neighbor, had purchased their farmhouse. Otto was instructed to sell the remaining livestock. The Starks had no use for the buildings at the time of the sale, so there was no need to empty them out. Otto sold Lucy's kitchen range, and left the goods in the house for future disposition, as well as storing some useful machinery in one of the unused buildings. All the money received from the live stock was accounted for and turned over to Mr. Redmond on his father's account, since the home property had been signed over in trust to Attorney Redmond at the onset of the involvement to keep the state from laying claim for prohibitive court costs.

On Monday, April 5, 1909, it was reported that City Attorney Redmond left Saturday for DesMoines to present before the board of pardons Joseph Usher's case; he felt that in the very near future Joseph Usher would be a free man.

# Chapter 45

## *SHERIFF'S SALE NOTICE*

By virtue of a special execution, directed to me, from the clerk of the district court, of Linn County, Iowa, on a judgment obtained in said court on the 16th day of April, 1909, in favor of John M. Ely and against Joseph A. Usher and Lucy J. Usher

*All for the sum of two thousand and seventy-three (2,073) dollars and fourteen (14) cents, and costs taxed at sixty-nine dollars and forty-eight cents, and accruing costs, I have levied upon the following real estate, personal property, taken as the property of said defendant to satisfy said execution, to-wit;*

*The north one-half (n1/2) of the northeast quarter (ne1/4) of the southeast quarter (se1/4) and the northeast quarter (ne1/4); all in section twenty eight (28) township eighty-three, (83), range eight (8), west of the fifth p.m. Linn county, Iowa.*

*And will offer the same for sale at public auction to the highest bidder for cash in hand on the 28th day of May,*

*A.D., 1909, in front of the court house door, in Marion, Linn county, Ia., at the hour of ten o'clock a.m., of said day when and where due attendance will be given by the undersigned. Dated at my office, in Marion, Iowa, this 26th day of April, 1909.*

W.G. Loftus,

Sheriff, of Linn County,

FRANK C. BYERS, Attorney.

# Chapter 46

Joseph Usher's family and their attorney had great reason to rejoice on Wednesday, May 5, 1909. At last Redmond could deliver good news to the Ushers, and he was overjoyed to do so: Joseph had been granted a pardon and was returning home on this very day. For Redmond, it was not every day that he came to care for his clients and their families, but in this case, he had come to care immensely, and the fight had been long enough for him to develop intimate relationships with the Ushers, and care about their future. For Attorney Redmond, this case had been particularly brutal, since the tragic murder of William Garrity had also been the undoing of the Usher family. They lost the female soul of their family, with the hospitalization of Lucy, and the inability to care for sweet little Linnie. He knew, they also lost the hub of their family, when Joseph was sent away to prison. Now Attorney Redmond longed to see this family heal, and find its way back to being united and strong.

Otto could hardly believe the story he was reading in *The Cedar Rapids Evening Gazette* on that day. He looked at the black inky print, staring at the words before him that he never thought he would see. Walter and he read the article back and forth to one another while their Grandma sat grinning in her chair, her hands pressed to her face. If only little Linnie and Lucy were here with them to celebrate and welcome Joseph back to the heart of their family.

*As the result of efforts that have been in progress for some time, Jos. Usher, born and raised in Linn County and for many years regarded as an industrious and enterprising citizen, was today released under parole from the Anamosa penitentiary, where he had served fifteen months for the alleged killing of Wm. Garrity, a hired man.*

*Mr. Usher returned at once to Cedar Rapids. He stated to a representative of the Gazette that he expects to so conduct himself that he will soon merit a full and complete pardon, of which there is absolutely no doubt.*

*The history of the Usher case is well known locally. Garrity was shot in the night, with a small target rifle.*

*The bedding on which he was sleeping was destroyed. Mr. Usher's peculiar actions gave rise to the suspicion that he had done the shooting. Although the evidence presented was purely circumstantial. He was convicted. The Supreme Court reversed the case. He was again convicted, being sentenced for eight years on the charge of manslaughter.*

*In a way, the case is one of the most pathetic in the annals of Linn County. For those who have followed every detail of the evidence do not believe that Mr. Usher is guilty. They believe that he held his tongue and suffers conviction and imprisonment rather than to lay the blame upon his wife. She is now in the asylum at Independence. She was then considered by many as mentally irresponsible.*

*Whether Mr. Usher will ever tell the true story of the tragedy is doubted, at least as long as his wife is alive.*

Otto put the newspaper down, took a deep breath and let out a sigh of relief. He was smiling as he announced. "It is finally over."

## OTTO'S INTERPRETATION OF EVENTS
## ON THE NIGHT OF THE MURDER
### Written by, Otto Usher, February 1, 1965

The morning of May 26, 1903, judging from my own reasoning and from what Dad told me after his release–I visualize the events about as follows:

That after l had gone to bed and to sleep some noise may have caused Dad to go upstairs to investigate the cause thereof. Seeing Bill there on the bed and bleeding. The rifle was nearby. He had become panicky and chucked the rifle out of sight.

He could have taken it out and thrown it in the empty granary–either before he wakened me, or more likely while I was gone down to the Spicer's. I went to make the telephone calls.

He would make no disclosures till necessary. In all probability the body would be washed off a bit. The slight hole made by so small a caliber gun would not be observed.

In fact this came quite near being what actually happened. The coroner testified at the trial that while he was washing off the body, he tried to wash what appeared to be a small hole under the blood, into which he could insert a small instrument. It was then that a doctor was called. A postmortem was preformed.

The bullet was traced thru the lung. It was found lodged in the eighth dorsal vertebra of the spine, thus causing a near instant paralysis and hemorrhage.

As I look back over these events. I can easily visualize what the ravages of fear can do to warp the judgment.

In any event it would have been so easy for Dad to have just left the gun by the side of the bed, come and called me. My Dad should have showed me the gun laying there. It was said by all that no one would have asked any questions.

If when the police took him in custody he had simply revealed that he had panicked and put the gun out of sight. Still I am sure no one would have tried to prove otherwise.

Dad should have told his lawyer just how it happened.

It still would have been an easy case. It would be a quite possible thing for a nervous man to do under the pressure. Of the then circumstances with Lucy as she was known to be. But he elected to keep it all to himself.

It seldom ever pays to do in this life as we are all much dependent on one another. It is much less confusing to lead an open life so all can see and understand. And I am sure we can better understand ourselves.

Some two or three years ago I learned Mr. Mekota the County Attorney was still alive. He was the County Attorney at the time all the litigation occurred.

I made an appointment with him, though he had long since been retired. I had a nice visit with him. He remembered most of the circumstances very well.

He told me that he was the first democrat ever elected in Linn County. He said he would not have been elected except for a certain circumstance of a rather amusing nature.

He asked me to come back and we would reminisce some more. I thought I might do that, however, soon after I learned that he had died.

I am reminded that someone should have said, Man should have two lives, so he could live his second life by the profit of his experience in the first one.

I hope these pages may clear up some of the conjectures anyone may have had about this subject I have dealt with.

These pages may be read by anyone or to anyone whom may be interested.

Yours Truly,
Otto Usher

# Afterword

During the transition years Otto started working for his Uncle Will. Usher March 1, 1906. After threshing season he received twenty-two dollars a month. That was the current rate and it included room and board.

At that time Otto visited his brother George and decided he, too, should farm. Otto would farm in Chickasaw County, near the towns of Ionia and Nashua, Iowa.

Otto had permission to have some of the house goods and the farm machinery from the old home place.

Otto traveled down to Cedar Rapids and out to the Weed home. Floyd helped Otto drive a team and wagon to the farm. The boys hauled the goods and machinery to town. They put them in a railroad car and shipped them up to Nashua.

When Joseph was released, Otto brought him back from Cedar Rapids to the farm home he was renting. Joseph was introduced to Otto's fiancée, Sylvia May De Graff, a lovely young woman from Chickasaw County. Otto and Sylvia were married September 29, 1909.

Walter settled in the same area as Otto and George. He was twenty- three when he married Justina Erickson March 8, 1917.

Joseph spent his last years living with his sons Otto, George and Walter.

My mother, Wilma Zubrod can remember her Grandfather,

249

Joseph Usher staying at Linnie's house. My mother was seven when her Grandfather, Joseph Usher Jr., passed away March 16, 1928 at the age of seventy-seven.

Lucy had had a complete mental breakdown when Joseph received a guilty verdict at the second trial. She was taken to the State Mental Hospital for the insane in Independence, Iowa. She was admitted May 19, 1906. She stayed until February 4, 1916. From there she was transferred to the county home where she stayed until August 5, 1921. She was then readmitted to the State Mental Hospital in Independence. She stayed there until her death March 19, 1944.

My mother told me that in March of 1944 her mother, Linnie asked her for a loan. In asking why, Linnie told her she needed the money to bury her mother, Lucy. Now this is the saddest part for my mother. Until this time my mother was raised to believe her Grandmother Lucy was dead. What a shock this must have been. I feel everyone's loss, and especially Lucy's–she must have been quite alone.

Mental illness in those days had quite a stigma and no one dealt with it. As a society, we have come a long way in accepting mental illness. However, we still have a long way to go.

Linnie was around five years old when she was sent to live with her mother's family. She said it was not an easy transition as she missed her father and brothers terribly.

I believe Linnie was turned to think against her mother. When my mother was expecting me she asked her mother, Linnie, what she should name her baby if she were a girl? Linnie responded, "What ever you do…don't name her Lucy." Her childhood did have an effect on her throughout the rest of her life.

Linnie Isabell Usher married Clarence Howard Blanchard at the age of seventeen, November 17, 1920. Clarence was twenty.

To this union five children were born:

–My mother Wilma May Zubrod, born May 13, 1921,

–Raymond Otis who lived less than a month, born February.11, 1923, died March 6, 1923,

–Marjorie Loraine Costello, Nixt, born March 6, 1926,

–Clara Velma Hartman, Murray, born November 19, 1927, died July 3, 1979,

–Leland Clarence Blanchard, born December 12, 1938.

Linnie found it difficult to accept the death of her first son.

My mother told me that in her early days her Mother, Linnie was very social. She was active in civic affairs and was progressive in her thinking. She helped my mother prepare to become a schoolteacher. My mother taught school until she married my father, Lloyd Zubrod. In those days you could not be married and teach school.

I remember my Grandmother Linnie as very quiet and kind. Mother used to take me to her little house in Nashua. I would give her a curly perm once a year. I know she appreciated our visit; however, when the perm was done it was time to go home.

As Linnie got older she became more reclusive. I feel some of this becoming reclusive was because of circumstances that occurred in her married life. That subject would be another story.

Linnie passed away from cancer September 9, 1981 at the age of seventy-seven years.

**Dear Reader,**

As I said in the beginning I began this story with love in my heart. Now that it is completed for me, my heart is overflowing with love for the characters. I have shed many tears in the telling of Lucy and Joseph's story.

I feel especially for Otto, whom I found to be an extraordinary son under extraordinary circumstances.

As Linnie's oldest granddaughter I went into this planning to defend Lucy. However, I have in my mind come to a different conclusion. Actually the whole truth will never be known, as Joseph and Lucy took the truth to their graves.

Lucy must have ranted and spoken the truth in her weak mental state. I feel that was the turn of events that caused Joseph's early release and pardon.

When we lived in the small town of Ionia, Iowa I was the hairdresser in that town. I actually did Otto's daughter, Alice Swinton's, hair. Alice was a very kind person and I liked her.

Do you know how you can feel when someone really likes you? That's how I sensed she felt about me. However, in the time I was doing her hair, she never once breathed even a hint that there was a story. I know I was not ready for this information at that time.

Alice actually sent me two notes at Christmas. I received the first note in 1992, the second in 1993. We had moved from Iowa in 1986 and were living in Florida. Now I wish I could speak to her about her father, Otto.

One of Otto's children asked him to write down some of the things he remembered. He started from the beginning with his childhood and continued through the murder.

From Otto's writings I had a wealth of information. Otto wrote his hand-written eighty- three page experiences about his life on February1, 1965.

I have so appreciated Otto's life story and his side of the events, which gave me a comparison of the issues and a wonderful view into his childhood.

From the thorough and excellent reporting of the local *Cedar Rapids* newspapers and the *Des Moines Daily News* I had over fifty-eight articles from which to draw.

These Newspapers are: *The Cedar Rapids Evening Gazette, The Cedar Rapids Daily Republican, The Cedar Rapids Republican, The Cedar Rapids Weekly Gazette, The Des Moines Daily News* and *The Nashua Reporter.*

My Uncle Leland Blanchard and his then wife Carol did a lot of the research on this subject. They went to the Usher reunions. At that time, the people who knew more of the story were still alive. They were fortunate to get to visit with them. I thank my Uncle Leland and Aunt Carol for all they did on this subject. And the valuable and time-consuming work they did with family genealogy.

My Mother, Wilma Zubrod has been able to help by talking to me. She was able to remember some of her mother Linnie's story of the early days. I believe my mother was one of the only ones Linnie told about the events in her childhood.

I remember my grandmother Linnie Blanchard very well.

I thank my husband Ron and my children Susie, Karen and Gary, and my daughter-in-law, Christine. They helped me with many thoughts and I appreciate their support. I thank my son-in-law, William Sudah, for his support and advice to write my story like a movie.

With love in my heart I end this story that I have had such a passion to write.

Nancy Panoch

# Otto's Reminiscences

## OTTO'S BROKEN ARM

*"Now comes to mind...it was while brother George, eight years older...was unloading some hay at the barn...he had told me to keep off the nearly empty hay wagon—did proceed to climb on regardless, when the front standard to the hay rack fell and pushed me down and broke my right arm just above the wrist...He and Mother hitched a "buggy" and started for town to the doctor. We met Father on the way home with the milk wagon, and so George drove the milk wagon on home while Father and Mother took me on into see old Dr. Carpenter. I recall I was afraid to take the chloroform, so they could set the bone, but Father promised if I would comply obediently that he would buy me a new tricycle—which he did, though I did not dare use it for a time—till my arm was quite healed."*

## INDIAN SQUAW STORY

*"It must have been at about this age that I recall one cold winter day while Mother and my sister, Jennie, were washing in the back kitchen...when a knock came at the door of the adjoining room—which was the front door. I went with Mother to see who it was, and there stood two Indian squaws, big and fat and scary-looking. Well their inquiry was as thus: Father*

had had the misfortune to have a very large hog get smoth-
ered by a portion of the straw stack, tipping over onto it a day
or so before, and they had just hauled it out and placed the
dead body out on a big snow bank, by the side of the road...
when the group of Indians, perhaps some fifteen or twenty of
them, observed it there...they sent the squaws back to inquire
how long it had been dead and if it had been sick. And when
Mother told them the circumstance, they wanted to know if
they could have it, and of course Mother was very glad to
have them take it off our hands. Father used to relate how
the Indians would go from the Iowa River area—south of our
place—and camp over on the Cedar River, near a high rock,
and make maple syrup in the early spring when the sap would
be flowing. He mentioned one instance that a group of his men
and boy friends sat with the Indians and helped keep the big
kettle boiling, till after midnight, that they might get a taste of
maple sugar and just about time...an old squaw came along
and spat in the kettle so the kids would not want any of the
sugar."

## JOSEPH'S COMMENT ABOUT OTTO ON WAY TOSCHOOL

"Might mention there was a creamery located across from
the school yard where Father hauled our milk on a sturdy
two-wheel cart with one horse. I recall one morning Father
overtook me on the way to the creamery, just as I reached
the schoolyard gate. I was feeling as I usually did on my way
to school the first few days. He casually remarked, so I could
hear, 'I wonder what nice little boy that could be?' To which I
replied, 'I guess you know who it is all right,' with considerable disgust."

## JOSEPH'S SCHOOL EXPERIENCE

*"Father's parents died when he was quite young, and he was sort of farmed out among the neighbors for a time until he could support himself...he went to school little, but, however, did learn to read and write and do simple sums in arithmetic. I recall standing beside his chair one evening, while he was reading the daily paper, and saying to him, 'I don't see any sense in setting there and looking at that paper.' He mentioned one of his school teachers, whom he had respected very much, a Mr. Ruder, that had previously made a trip around the world, a very unusual thing to have done in those days. He related recalling that this teacher, having been informed that the school had been very disorderly under previous tutoring, had on the...way to school the first morning...cut and trimmed a fine hickory stick and placed it in plain sight over the blackboard. And when school opened that first morning, he explained to the pupils that he was only going to have one rule, and that was it right up there where everybody could see. He said they did have a very good order and learned a great deal under the tutoring of this fine man."*

## OTTO MILKING WITH HIS FATHER

*'I went with Father on the milk route quite often—except on school days—of course. There were some rewarding experiences of course. Father was a very early riser in the morning. I can still recall how on very cold wintry mornings his making a sort of yelping noise like a dog, which I presume may have had a dual purpose, one which may have been to invigorate and warm himself to meet the cold, and the other to awaken George and I, and the hired man when we had one. I*

*began to help with the milking when I was about nine or ten years old. I suppose—though I do not remember specifically."*

## ENGLISH BOYS

*'I suppose it was about this time when Father had contacted an agency in town whose purpose it was to find people who would except the responsibility of receiving young English men into their homes, and try and help them acquaint themselves to the American way of life. These fellows had had schooling at home, but needed counsel and a guiding hand till they could get themselves adjusted to the ways of a very new environment to them. I vaguely recall the first one or two of these boys, one by the name of King (I may have a photo of him) who came first. I recall Father telling how we were in harvest time, and that they were shocking oats, and this fellow came out from the house to help...dressed in a heavy brocade cloth suit, which was black, and it was a very hot day so Father advised him to go back to the house and get one something cooler...which he did...this time, he appeared in a white linen. Now of course this...was very amusing to brother George, whom may have been about fifteen years old at that time. Well of course many awkward situations were encountered, amusing to the younger natives, but very dis-concerting to these poor fellows in a strange new country. Some times young folks can be rather cruel in dealing with situations of such kind...quite unintentional of course. Well this fellow did not stay very long, and we soon lost all mind of him."*

## OTTO, FLOYD WEED AND MUSIC

'It was about at this period of time that Floyd Weed and I each decided that we would try a bit of music…well we each purchased a violin, or a fiddle, if you please, and started taking lessons from a Mrs. Richardson…she and her husband played with the Ureene's Opera House Orchestra; we contacted her because we know her as a girl who grew up in the neighborhood. She and two brothers being some older…she was a fine musician. At that time, however, I guess neither one of us boys were of the musical strain, and after about a dozen lessons, we must have decided that being a violinist was not attained without much work and devotion, and besides—I presume other interests diverted our thoughts to other fields of interest.'

## OTTO AND CHURCH

'It was during these years while I was about fourteen years old that I found myself living—or shall I say struggling—between two different influences in the same neighborhood. There were the ones that went to church on Sunday and took an active part in the church work. They were very good to me and I am very thankful for them. I recall going to church with them one Sunday, and near the close of the service, Mr. Weed came over where Floyd and I were sitting, and told Floyd that he wished him to go forward and make the good confession–which he did at that time. Where upon Floyd's older sister came to where I were sitting and wanted me to go along with him. While I was sure it was the proper thing to do, something seemed to hold me and say, 'there would be a more convenient season.' Well of course there are many impulses to recall. I liked to be with *the other group because they liked to hunt and fish and go to shows, then they had a steam engine with their threshing rig, which intrigued me almost to the point of idolatry. As silly as it may seem, while they smoked and chewed tobacco and drank lots of beer, I don't remember that they ever offered any to me...neither do I recall that I had so much of a desire to indulge...though I don't know why, but for which I am very thankful now of course."*

## Nashua Reporter March 21, 1928

### Joseph Usher's Obituary

Joseph Aaron Usher Jr. was born in Linn Co., Iowa December 24, 1850. He departed this life at the home of his son Otto March 16, 1928. Mr. Usher died at the age of seventy-seven years two months and twenty-one days.

He was married to Miss Mary Suzanna Peal in 1873 at Cedar Rapids, Iowa.

To this union four children were born. They are Mrs. Mary Jane Dudley of Santa Monica, California, Walter of Bassett and George and Otto of Nashua.

His wife preceded him in death August 6, 1898.

April 11, 1900 he was again united in marriage to Miss Lucy Gillis of Centerville, Iowa. To this union one daughter was born, Linnie, Mrs. Clarence Blanchard of Nashua.

Besides the children, he is survived by two brothers, William of Republic, Iowa and Isaac of Clarinda, Iowa. There are twenty-two grandchildren. Four Grandchildren preceded him in death.

For twenty years the deceased was a very successful farmer of Linn Co. He owned a large dairy farm. He left there some years ago to be near his children. The children had come to Chickasaw County to establish their homes.

About fifteen years ago he united with the Methodist Church at Republic. He remained a member until his death.

For the last three years Mr. Usher had been in very poor health. Ten days ago he was taken ill with organic heart disease. From which he gradually grew weaker until he passed to eternal rest to be with his lord.

Funeral services were held at the Methodist Church, Nashua. Sunday, March 18. Rev A.Raymond Grant was officiating. The body was taken to Cedar Rapids by Undertaker Lundt for interment.

# References

The Cedar Rapids Evening Gazette, 5-27, 1903, p. 2. - 5-28, 1903, p. 1. 3. - 5-30, 1903, p. 5. - 6-1, 1903, p. 5. - 6-2, 1903, p. 5. 6-4, 1903, p. 3. - 6-5, 1903, p. 2. - 6-6, 1903, p. 6. - 6-16, 1903, p. 5. - 6-23, 1903, p. 5.- 6-29, 1903, p. 8. - 10-10, 1903, p. 8. - 10-30, 1903, vol. 21. n. 252. p1. - 10-31, 1903, p.8. 11-13, 1903, p. 5. - 11-4, 1903, p. 2& 8. - 11-6, 1903, p. 1. - 11-9, 1903, p. 1.2&5. - 11-10, 1903, vol. 21 no. 261, p.1&4. - 11-13, 1903, p. 5. - 1-10, 1905, p. 2. - 1-11, 1905, p.5&10. - 9-19, 1908, continued from page 27. - 4-20, 1909, p.10. - 4-27, 1909, Notices. - 5-5, 1909, p. 11. - 7-15, 1910, p. 3.

Cedar Rapids Weekly Gazette, 6-17, 1903, p. 6. - 7-1, 1903, p. 8. - 10-14, 1903, p. 5. - 3-2, 1904, p. 4. - 5-10, 1904, p. 1. - 12-14, 1904, p. 12. - 1-18, 1905, p.7. - 5-23, 1906, p. 7.

The Cedar Rapids Republican, 5-28, 1903, p. 1. - 5-30, 1903, p. 6. - 11-5, 1903, no. 213 p.1. - 11-6, 1903, p.1. – 11- 11, 1903, vol. 33 no. 217, p.1. - 11-12, 1903, vol. 33 no. 218. – 11- 13, 1903, vol. 33 no. 219, p.1.

The Cedar Rapids Gazette, 11- 11, 1903 vol. 21, p.1.

The Cedar Rapids Daily Republican, 5- 29, 1903, p.1&6.

- 6- 3, 1903, p. 2. - 6- 23, 1903, p. 8. - 10-10, 1903, p. 6. - 1-12, 1905, p. 1. 5- 12, 1906, p.1. - 5-19, 1906, p. 5. - 5-8, 1907, p. 5. - 1-10, 1908, see inside page.

The Cedar Rapids Sunday Republican, 6-7, 1903, p. 4.

The Des Moines Daily Capital, 1-11, 1905, p. 5. - 5-19, 1906, p. 3.

The Des Moines Daily News, 5-19, 1906, p. 5. - 9-2, 1906, p. 3.

Nashua Reporter, 3- 21, 1928.

Otto Usher's Eighty-Three Page Hand-Written Record of His Life, 2- 1, 1965.

The Usher family's early written records of the Usher family's history.